英汉对照管理丛书 9

心理测试
PSYCHOMETRIC TESTING
Pocketbook

【英】巴里·克里普斯博士 & 多萝西·斯普赖 著
（Dr Barry Cripps & Dorothy Spry）

菲尔·黑尔斯顿（Phil Hailstone） 绘图

胡莉明 译

上海交通大学出版社
SHANGHAI JIAO TONG UNIVERSITY PRESS

内容提要

　　本书为"英汉对照管理丛书"之一，主要介绍了如何在工作中使用心理测试，如何选择测试，并分别介绍了组织发展测试、团队测试、个人发展测试、职业咨询测试等不同类型的测试。本书为英汉对照，便于读者在学习管理的同时学到地道的英文表达。

© Dr Barry Cripps & Dorothy Spry 2008

This translation of Psychometric Testing Pocketbook first published in 2015 is published by arrangement with Management Pocketbooks Limited

版权合同登记号：图字：09-2013-720 号

图书在版编目（CIP）数据

心理测试／（英）克里普斯（Crips, B.），（英）斯普赖（Spry, D.）著；胡莉明译 . —上海：上海交通大学出版社，2015
（英汉对照管理丛书）
ISBN 978-7-313-12332-9

Ⅰ．心…　Ⅱ．①克…　②斯…　③胡…　Ⅲ．心理测验－英、汉　Ⅳ．B841.7

中国版本图书馆 CIP 数据核字（2014）第 266320 号

心理测试

著　　者：［英］巴里·克里普斯　　　　　译　　者：胡莉明
　　　　　多萝西·斯普赖
出版发行：上海交通大学出版社　　　　　地　　址：上海市番禺路 951 号
邮政编码：200030　　　　　　　　　　　电　　话：021-64071208
出 版 人：韩建民
印　　制：常熟市文化印刷有限公司　　　经　　销：全国新华书店
开　　本：880mm×1230mm 1/32　　　　印　　张：7.875
字　　数：196 千字
版　　次：2015 年 1 月第 1 版　　　　　印　　次：2015 年 1 月第 1 次印刷
书　　号：ISBN 978-7-313-12332-9/B
定　　价：28.00 元

编辑的话

嗨，大家好！

最早出版这个系列的书（英汉对照管理袖珍手册）是在 2002 年，随后我们又在 2004 年和 2007 年分别推出了第二辑和第三辑。这套丛书（共 50 本）被很多 500 强企业用作培训教材，也被很多读者整套收藏。

这一次，我们对书的开本做了调整。我们给您留出了做笔记的空间。您可以把您查阅的英文单词、词组和句式写在原文下面空白的 Notes 处，也可以把您阅读过程中的所思所想写在此处，把这本书真正变成属于您自己的书。

另外，我们对中文字体也作了调整，让您阅读起来更为轻松。

因为这些调整，书不再那么袖珍，所以丛书名也改为了"英汉对照管理丛书"。

如果您有什么建议和反馈，请别忘了告诉我们！（请发邮件至：wangliatcn@qq.com）

再一次，祝您阅读愉快！

汪俪
2014 年 12 月

FROM THE AUTHORS

The very words **psychometric** and **testing** can be enough to clear a room, and sound sufficiently alarming to prevent many people from considering using tests in the first place. In addressing this topic it is not our intention to give you a headache, or swamp you with too many scientific and statistical facts.

Instead, we are keen to introduce the non-specialist reader to the world of psychometric testing in as practical and user-friendly a way as possible. This pocketbook is written for managers in human resources, line managers, administrators and anyone who needs to know about workplace testing in all its forms. Further reading references are provided at the end of the book for individuals who wish to delve more deeply into the scientific background behind each test mentioned.

作者的话

单是**"心理测量学"**和**"测试"**这两个词就足以吓跑所有人了，听起来让人害怕，一开始就不愿意使用测试。我们谈论这个话题并不打算给您增添烦恼，也不打算丢给您成堆的科学事实和数据。

相反，我们期望用尽可能实用的、用户友好的方式，引导非专业读者了解心理测试。本书面向人力资源经理、部门经理、管理人员以及任何需要了解职场测试的人。书末有延伸阅读和参考书目，供读者深入了解书中所提到测试的科学背景。

目　录

CONTENTS

INTRODUCTION

简 介

> "To test or not to test, that is the question…
> … and then, which test to use?"

> "要不要心理测试，这是个问题……
> 其次，使用哪种测试呢？"

INTRODUCTION

AIM OF THIS POCKETBOOK

The aim of this pocketbook is to act as a practical guide, taking you step by step through the process of selecting the most appropriate psychometric test or tests, in order to provide your own workplace solutions.

We will start by introducing a workplace scenario, looking at what the organisation needs to achieve, and then explain how the testing can be used to bring this about. A mixture of popular psychometric tests has been selected and will be supported by a range of situational case studies for the following areas:

- Selection
- Promotion
- Managing your team and team development
- Personal development: growing potential in the individual
- Career counselling and development

This book is **not** about:

- ✗ Training you to use tests – though we do suggest ways to become fully trained
- ✗ Recommending any specific test – we do, however, demonstrate commonly used tests
- ✗ Fully reviewing any particular test – but we do show you how to obtain full test reviews

Notes

_____

_____

_____

_____

_____

本书的目的

　　本书意在成为一本实用向导，带领读者一步步选择最合适的一个或多个心理测试，从而提供你个人的职场解决方案。

　　我们开始会先介绍职场情境，看看组织需要实现的目标是什么，再解释如何利用测试实现目标。我们挑出了一些颇受欢迎的心理测试组合，并将结合以下方面的情景进行实例分析：

- 遴选
- 晋升
- 管理团队和团队发展
- 个人发展：发展个人潜力
- 职业咨询和发展

这本书**不是**：

✘ 培训你使用测试——尽管我们给出了关于如何充分接受培训的建议

✘ 推荐具体某个测试——虽然我们展示了经常使用到的测试

✘ 充分评价具体某个测验——但是我们会告诉您如何获取全面的测试评价

BENEFITS OF TESTING TO YOUR ORGANISATION

Some of the benefits of using a good psychometric test or tests to assess people are that they give results that are:

- Objective – not influenced by personal feelings or opinions
- Systematic – working to a fixed plan
- Reliable – able to be trusted, because they are consistent across administrations and sample groups
- Valid – measures of what the tests set out to measure

The individual benefits from equality and fairness of treatment for all test takers. All candidates are being assessed against each other, under controlled conditions, regardless of gender, diversity of background and age.

Notes

_____

_____

_____

_____

_____

测试对组织的好处

使用一个或多个良好的心理测试来评价员工所带来的好处在于它们给出的结果：

- 客观——不受个人情感或意见的影响
- 系统——按既定的计划行事
- 可靠——可以信赖，因为结果不随实施者和样本团队而改变
- 有效——能够测出测试本身要达到的结果

对所有测试对象一视同仁，测试对象将从中受益。所有测试者在受控制的条件下，不论性别、背景和年龄，进行单独测试。

BENEFITS OF TESTING TO YOUR ORGANISATION

Testing can help you to:

- Identify applicants with the potential to fit job demands and be high performers (recruitment, selection and promotion)
- Aid understanding of individuals and team members and their possible interaction (personal and team development)
- Improve the motivation and morale of those tested, through acknowledgement of their contribution to success (organisational development)
- Increase retention – using your knowledge and understanding of staff's strengths to place them in appropriate functions
- Develop benchmarks – to identify star performers
- Clearly demonstrate fairness and equal opportunities for all
- Demonstrate consistency over time – using reliable and valid methods of assessment
- Reduce time, costs and mismatches in recruitment and selection – adding to the bottom-line
- Assist with group training and individual coaching
- *Read the pulse* before and after major organisational change – eg downsizing, acquisitions and mergers

Notes

_____

_____

_____

_____

_____

简介

测试对组织的好处

测试能够帮助你：

- 筛选出可能符合工作要求、工作效率高的申请者（招聘、遴选、晋升）

- 了解个人、团队成员及他们之间可能产生的相互作用（个人和团队发展）

- 通过认可被测试者对成功做出的贡献，提升他们的积极性和士气（组织发展）

- 增加员工留住率——运用你对员工优势的认识和了解，使员工各得其所

- 完善考核标准——选出表现杰出者

- 清晰展示对所有人的平等对待和公平机会

- 证明一致性，不随时间变化——采用可靠、有效的评估方法

- 减少招聘和遴选的时间、成本并减少错误匹配——增加管理效率

- 有助于团体培训和个人教练

- 反映企业重大变革前后的"脉搏"——如裁员、收购和兼并

INTRODUCTION

DEFINITION

Put simply, psychometric means 'mental measurement', so a psychometric test can measure aspects of the individual such as ability, personality, motivation, competencies, behaviours and interests.

The word test is generic: it is applied generally to all instruments. Some 'tests' are not tests *per se*, so we interchangeably use words like questionnaire, inventory, tool, assessment or instrument.

'A psychological test is any procedure on the basis of which inferences are made concerning a person's capacity, propensity or liability to act, react, experience, or to structure or order thought or behaviour in particular ways.'
The British Psychological Society

Notes

_____

_____

_____

_____

_____

定义

　　简单来说，心理测试就是"心理评估"，所以心理测试能测试一个人的才能、人格、动机、胜任力、行为和兴趣等方面。

　　"测试"这个词是泛指的：通常适用于所有工具。一些"测试"本身不是测试，所以我们交替使用像问卷、量表、工具、评估或手段这样的词。

> "心理测试指做出推断的过程，是一个人的能力、习性，或行为、反应、经验方面的倾向，或者以某种方式组织、排列想法、行为的倾向。"
> ——英国心理学会

INTRODUCTION

WHAT MAKES A GOOD PSYCHOMETRIC TEST?
A GOOD TEST HAS MUSCLE & ENDURANCE

There are two main types of psychometric tests used in the workplace:

- Tests of **maximum** performance, ie general ability tests
- Tests of **typical** performance, ie personality or interest inventories

The British Psychological Society has set up a certificate scheme for test users: the Level A and B Certificates of Competence in Occupational Testing. The authors recommend that all test users seek certification in test use in order to maintain professional standards. Details are given at the end of this pocketbook.

A well constructed test goes together with the ingredients of reliability and validity like honey goes with bees. You cannot have one without the other.

Notes

_____

_____

_____

_____

简介

什么是好的心理测试？

好的测试具备肌肉和耐力

职场上使用的心理测试主要有两种：

- **最佳**绩效测试，即一般能力测试
- **典型**绩效测试，即人格量表或兴趣量表

英国心理学会为测试用户制定了一个认定体系：A 级和 B 级职业测试能力证明。为保持专业标准，作者推荐所有测试用户获得使用测试的能力证明。本书末尾有详细介绍。

正如有蜜蜂才有蜂蜜，一个结构完善的测试所具备的要素包括信度、效度，二者缺一不可。

蜂蜜

INTRODUCTION

SELECTING THE RIGHT TEST

It is no exaggeration to say that the market place is flooded with psychometric tests (10,000 at a low estimate!). Many produce professional looking reports that at first sight can appear impressive. Some of these tests, however, may not carry a robust body of research behind them in order to satisfy high reliability and validity.

Any good test should be fully researched and rigorously tested before being let loose in the marketplace and made available to the largely unsuspecting general public.

Cautionary tale:
An unfortunate HR officer bought an off-the-shelf psychometric test to use when recruiting for a sales position. The test was supposed to identify a positive, self-starting, confident and extravert person. How come they ended up with someone full of doom and gloom?

Answer: although the test stated that it could measure the above positive attributes, it was not valid, failing to measure what it purported to measure, with potentially disastrous consequences.

Notes

选择恰当的测试

毫不夸张地说，市面上的心理测试已泛滥成灾。（估计至少有10,000 种！）许多测试生成的报告乍看起来很不错，但是，其中一些测试并没有坚实的研究基础，信度和效度都不高。

任何好的测试在投放市场之前，都应该经过充分研究和严格测试，然后才能给不知情的大众使用。

警示故事：

一名倒霉的人力资源职员购买了一套现成的心理测试表，并用来招聘销售岗位。这套测试本来应该筛选出积极主动、自信外向的人，为什么最后选出来的却是悲观沮丧的人呢？

答案：这个测试声称能测出以上积极特征，但由于没有效度，无法达到它声称的测量效果，造成了潜在的严重后果。

INTRODUCTION

INGREDIENTS OF A GOOD TEST

To help avoid the pitfalls of selecting an inappropriate psychometric test, here is a checklist of core questions to ask:

✔ Is there a user's guide or technical manual stating what statistical trials the test has been through and explaining how to administer, score, analyse and interpret?

✔ Has the test been trialled on a large (well over 500) representative sample of people?

✔ What is the test's reliability strength? Does it give consistent results, day after day? You can easily check by reading the research and looking at the test review at the British Psychological Society psychometric testing website – **www.psychtesting.org.uk**

✔ Has the test been validated across cultures, occupations, age and gender and norms produced for each group? Any valid test measures what it purports to measure, eg an aspect of self such as ability, personality, behaviour, intelligence, motivation or aptitude

✔ Are faking detectors built in to check for signs of manipulation from the test taker?

When choosing any test, it is essential that it matches a careful job analysis of the attributes actually required to do the job. **Look beyond the glossy cover of any test.**

Notes

_____

_____

_____

_____

_____

简介

好的测试所具备的要素

为了避免选到一套不恰当的心理测试，这里列出了一个核心要点清单：

✔ 是否有用户指南或技术手册，清楚说明对这套测试进行的统计试验，以及如何实施、计分、分析和阐释？

✔ 这套测试是否针对大的样本代表人群(500 人以上)进行过试验？

✔ 这套测试的可信度如何？是否在不同时候给出的结果都一致？你可通过查阅英国心理学会心理测试网站——www.psychtesting.org.uk 上的评论进行核对。

✔ 这套测试是否经过不同文化、职业、年龄和性别群体的验证，并且针对每个群体都生成了规范？任何有效的测试都能够测出它所声称能测试的内容，如能力、人格、行为、智力、动机或能力倾向。

✔ 是否嵌入了欺骗识别题来检查受测者的操控迹象？

无论挑选任何测试，都要与实际工作需求的属性相匹配，这是至关重要的。**不要光看测试的表面。**

INTRODUCTION

GOOD PRACTICE

Test takers have a right to know:

- How their results will be used and interpreted
- Whether the test users are competent to score and interpret results
- How test scores will be communicated and to whom
- Who will have access to results
- How confidentiality will be protected
- How long test scores will be stored
- What assurances will be given to ensure that test scores are not used for purposes other than those agreed with the test taker
- What feedback will be given
- That the tests are properly constructed

Test takers should be given a contact name or phone number if there are any questions or issues to be raised. In team settings, team members should agree how their results should be shared amongst each other with respect only to making the team more efficient.

Notes

_____

_____

_____

_____

_____

簡介

良好的做法

测试对象有权知道：

- 他们的测试结果将如何被使用和解释
- 测试使用者是否有能力给出得分、解释结果
- 测试得分如何被告知，告知给谁
- 谁能够看到结果
- 如何维持保密性
- 测试得分会保留多久
- 如何保证除了测试对象同意的用途，这些结果不会被用于其他用途
- 会给出什么反馈
- 测试的结构是完善的

为避免出现任何问题或情况，应将联系人的姓名或电话提供给测试对象。对于团队，为了令团队更加高效，团队成员对如何共享彼此的测试结果应达成统一意见。

INTRODUCTION

GOOD PRACTICE

Tests should never be used as a sole means of making personnel decisions because:

- A single measure of a person only looks at that person in one way, from one perspective. This may not be enough in the complex nature of work today. Ability or personality is not everything at work; motivation, interests, sociability, emotional intelligence, track record, experience are all important and need to be taken into account

- All tests are subject to error, and can never be 100% accurate. Error occurs in the way that candidates interpret the words in the questions, error exists in the person, error will occur in the test administration and differences in scores have been noticed according to the time of day of testing. One reason untrained people should not use psychological tests is that they may not understand 'error of measurement' and place too much emphasis on accuracy of test results

After all, a tailor or dressmaker needs considerably more than one set of measurements to make a well-fitting garment.

Notes

_____

_____

_____

_____

_____

良好的做法

绝不应该把测试作为人事决策的唯一手段，因为：

• 一个测试只是以某种方式、从某个角度来观察一个人，对于现今工作的复杂性质是不够的。能力或人格不是工作的所有方面；动机、兴趣、交际能力、情绪智力、业绩记录和经验这些都很重要，也要考虑进去。

• 所有的测试都有可能出错，绝不可能百分之百准确。有可能是应试者理解错了问题中的词语，错误产生于那个人，也可能因为测试管理员，而且由于测试时间的不同，测试结果也会不同。未受过培训的人不应该使用心理测试的原因之一就是他们可能不理解"测量误差"，过于强调测试结果的准确性。

毕竟，裁缝要做出合身的衣服，需要进行多种测量。

TESTING FOR SELECTION

遴选测试

WHY USE SELECTION TESTS?

The rationale behind using tests in selection is the better an individual performs on a test, the better that individual will perform in the workplace.

In this chapter we will look at a few scenarios in which selection tests can be used effectively when recruiting or selecting people for a job. It needs to be very clear that the skills tested must be specifically applicable in the job. For instance, when selecting a PA it would not be appropriate to test for mechanical or spatial ability.

Tests should not be used on their own, as a sole basis for hiring people, and should never ever be used for the purpose of firing people!

Notes

_____

_____

_____

_____

_____

遴选测试

为什么使用遴选测试?

　　使用测试进行人员遴选的理由和根据是一个人的某项测试结果越好，他在职场上就会表现得越好。

　　这一章我们来看一看能够在招聘或选择岗位候选人时使用遴选测试的一些场景。必须确定的一点是，测试的技能必须专门适用于那项工作，如挑选私人助理时，测试机械能力或空间能力是不适合的。

　　不应该单独使用测试，并将其作为招聘时的唯一基础，并且，绝不能用其来解雇人！

TESTING FOR SELECTION

INTELLIGENCE TESTS

Intelligence testing, as a concept, is not generally used in business, but we feel it is useful to discuss it briefly as it forms the basis of ability testing in general.

The concept of the Intelligence Quotient (IQ) was fashionable about fifty years ago and used, for instance, in selecting children at 11+ to enter grammar school. The national average IQ score is 100, so a child who gained a score of 120 would be 20 points above average, and would normally have expected to secure a place at the grammar school.

Testing for **intelligence** in occupational applications like selection is not that useful because of the alarming fact that intelligence peaks at around 17 years of age.

Testing for **ability** is the next best alternative and it is generally recognised that if you have only a short time to assess an applicant for a job, the best way to use that time is to give the applicant an ability test.

Notes

遴选测试

智力测试

　　作为一个概念，智力测试通常不用在商务领域，但因为它基本上是能力测试的基础，我们有必要简单讲一下。

　　智商（IQ）这个概念在大约 50 年前很流行，例如在挑选 11 岁以上的孩子进入文法学校时会使用，全英国的 IQ 平均分是 100，分数为 120 的孩子比平均分高 20，通常有望顺利进入文法学校。

　　在类似人员遴选的职业应用当中，针对**智力**的测试并不是非常有用，因为事实上人在 17 岁左右时智力是最高的。

　　针对**能力**的测试是次佳选择。通常认为，如果只有很短的时间来评估某个岗位的应聘者，最好利用那段时间让他进行能力测试。

TESTING FOR SELECTION

USING ABILITY TESTS FOR SELECTION

It can often be very difficult to identify the range of abilities a person possesses when they apply for a job. It can be harder still if they have no formal qualifications, or are applying for a first job or a supervisory or management position for the first time. Ability, in this context, is a level of mental power: the capacity to do something like reading or mental arithmetic.

Ability tests measure an individual's special abilities; for example how well a candidate works with words or numbers. If someone applies for a job in a bank working with figures, a test of numerical ability would highlight their suitability for the job. Or, when recruiting for a trainee airline pilot, it would be important to test applicants for their spatial awareness ability, so that they can land on the correct runway (!), and to look at their logical reasoning, problem solving and stress management abilities.

We are going to highlight a few of these areas by providing case studies of how tests can be used practically within an organisational setting.

Notes

遴选测试

使用能力测试进行遴选

通常，应聘者申请某个岗位时，辨别他们所具备的能力范畴是很困难的。如果应聘者没有正式的资格认证，或者应聘的是第一份工作，或第一次申请督导岗或管理岗，就会更加困难。在这里，能力是指脑力水平：即做某事的能力，如阅读或心算。

能力测试测量的是一个人的具体能力：例如应聘者对于词语或数字的处理能力怎样。如果某人申请的是银行的工作，要和数字打交道，测试他的算术能力就能看出他是否适合那份工作。或者，招聘航空飞行员实习生时，测试应聘者的空间意识能力是很重要的，这样他们才能准确地降落在跑道上！并且要看看他们的逻辑推理能力、解决问题能力和压力管理能力。

我们将给出一些案例研究，说明怎么把测试实际应用到组织中。

TESTING FOR SELECTION

THE GOLDEN TRIANGLE

The Golden Triangle in testing for selection:

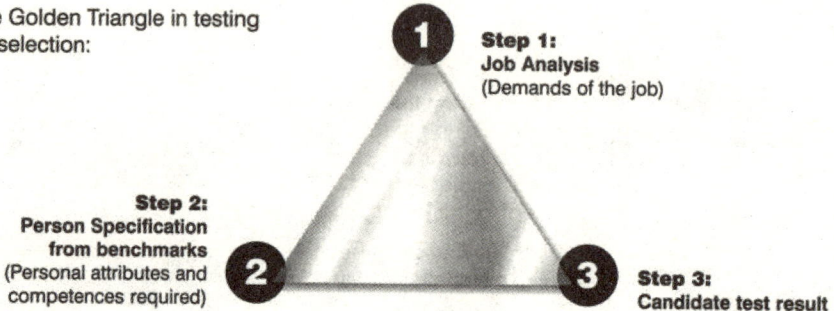

Step 1:
Job Analysis
(Demands of the job)

Step 2:
Person Specification
from benchmarks
(Personal attributes and competences required)

Step 3:
Candidate test result

In choosing which tests to use, you want to select those that come closest to matching the competences required by the Job Analysis and Person Specification, and matching the person into the job framework.

Notes

遴选测试

金三角

遴选测试中的金三角：

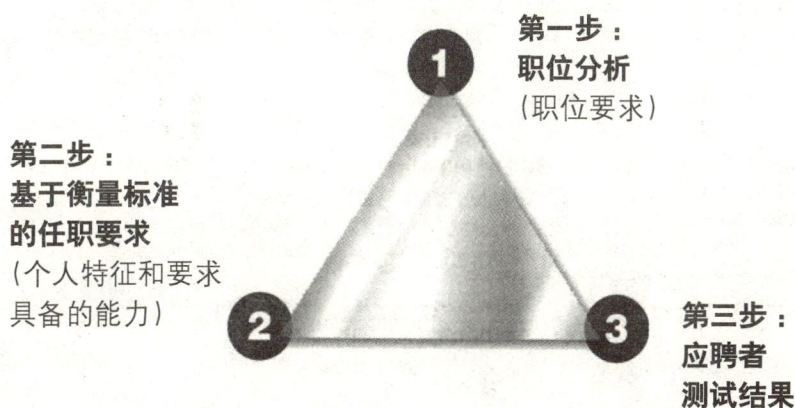

第一步：
职位分析
（职位要求）

第二步：
基于衡量标准
的任职要求
（个人特征和要求
具备的能力）

第三步：
应聘者
测试结果

　　在选择使用哪个测试时，您希望的是根据职位分析和任职要求，选出最匹配这些能力的人，把这个人安排到岗位体系中。

TESTING FOR SELECTION

GENERAL ABILITY TESTS (GAT 2)
CASE STUDY

A nationwide bakery had for many years been using the **General Ability Tests** (GAT 2 Verbal and Numerical) as part of their recruitment process. After conducting an internal review of the company's use of psychometrics for selection and development, a decision was made to undertake a study involving the bakery's 45 area and production managers. The purpose was to collect a batch of in-house 'norms' and to look at how the tests predicted workplace performance. Norms are established by obtaining a representative sample of successful job holders' scores on GAT2. These scores are then used as a benchmark for the comparison of future job applicants' test scores against those of successful incumbent individuals.

To assure existing employees of the confidentiality of the testing process, an external organisation was called in to process the test results and undertake the data analysis.

There are five GAT2 tests which make up the battery of tests for ability. The tests give a clear indication of an individual's general intellectual ability regardless of education or previous experience.

Used with the kind permission of ASE.

Notes

遴选测试

一般能力测试（GAT 2）

案例研究

一家全国性的面包店多年来一直使用**一般能力测试**（GAT2语言和数字），并将其作为招聘过程的一部分。公司内部针对公司所使用的选择和发展心理测试进行商讨后，决定对面包店包括的45个地区和产品经理进行一项调查，目的是收集一套内部"规范"，观察测试对职场表现的预测效果。这些规范是根据优秀职员在GAT2中的得分所形成的代表性样本而创建的，然后把这些得分作为以后的应聘者测试分数和在职人员的对比基准。

为确保现有雇员测试的保密性，外部聘请了公司进行结果处理和数据分析。

针对能力的系列测试包括五个GAT2测试。这些测试能清楚地反映个人的一般智力，而不论其教育背景和以往经历如何。

经 ASE 允许使用。

GENERAL ABILITY TESTS (GAT 2)
CASE STUDY

The five GAT2 tests are:

1. **Verbal** – Measures the ability to reason with words through the use of analogies (used in this study to gather internal norms).

2. **Non-Verbal** – Measures the ability to process information, recognise relationships and differentiate between relevant and irrelevant information.

3. **Numerical** – Measures the ability to identify relationships between numbers but without the need for extensive mathematical knowledge (used in this study to gather internal norms).

4. **Spatial** – Measures the ability to visualise objects in 3D (ideal when assessing for positions which involve the manipulation of 3D objects).

5. **Mechanical** – Measures the ability to visualise relationships between moving parts and the way in which mechanical systems operate.

The tests can be administered individually, or in any combination, as in this case.

Used with the kind permission of ASE.

Notes

遴选测试

一般能力测试（GAT 2）

案例研究

5 个 GAT2 测试是：

(1) **语言**——通过使用类比，测量语言推理能力（在本次调查中用来收集内部规范）。

(2) **非语言**——测量处理信息的能力、关系识别能力和分辨相关信息与无关信息的能力。

(3) **数字**——测量对数字之间关系的识别能力，但不要求有全面的数学知识（在本次调查中用来收集内部规范）。

(4) **空间**——测量三维空间的想象能力（非常适于评估涉及 3D 物体操作的岗位）。

(5) **机械**——测量对移动物体间关系及以哪种机械方式运转的想象力。

这些测试可以单独使用，也可像本案例中一样组合使用。

经 ASE 允许使用。

GENERAL ABILITY TESTS (GAT 2)

CASE STUDY: CONCLUSION

The assessments are presented in a 'text free' format. The scores are not influenced by reading comprehension and are therefore fairer to individuals from different cultures or educational backgrounds.

The outcome of the study showed there to be a significant relationship between performance on both the Verbal and Numerical tests and performance on the job. The bakery is now continuing to collect relevant on-going test data to add to their internal norms. Furthermore, they have now fully integrated the GAT2 test battery into their recruitment processes. Both recruitment and retention in the company have been improved by using these norms as benchmarks.

Next we will look at aptitude tests.

Notes

_____

_____

_____

_____

_____

_____

遴选测试

一般能力测试（GAT 2）

案例研究：结论

评估的呈现形式"不含文本"，得分不会因为阅读能力的不同而受到影响，因此对于来自不同文化背景或教育背景的人来说很公平。

调查结果显示，语言和数字这两项测试的结果与工作表现有显著联系。面包店正在继续收集持续进行的测试的数据，并将其添加到他们的内部规范当中。此外，他们已经把 GAT2 系列测试充分融入到招聘过程中。通过利用这些规范作为基准，公司的招聘和员工保持率都得到了改善。

下面来看能力倾向测试。

TESTING FOR SELECTION

APTITUDE TESTS

An aptitude is a natural ability to be good at something, eg hand-eye co-ordination for juggling, or ball skills for tennis. An aptitude test predicts how good someone is likely to be at acquiring a new skill or body of knowledge, determining a person's ability in that skill *(Cook & Cripps, 2005)* such as learning a new computer skill.

Sometimes aptitude tests can be combined to form a multiple aptitude battery such as the Computer Programmers Aptitude Battery, which is ideal for assessing computer programmers and systems analysts. This test will be highlighted in the following case study.

You may notice that the use of the words **ability** and **aptitude** by test publishers is very finely drawn and may overlap. This fine distinction takes nothing away from the actual tests.

Notes

_____

_____

_____

_____

_____

遴选测试

能力倾向测试

　　能力倾向是与生俱来擅长做某事的能力，如杂耍的手眼协调能力，或网球技能。能力倾向测试可以预测某人掌握某个技能或知识的可能性，决定一个人在某项技能方面的能力（库克＆克里普斯，2005），例如，学习一项新的电脑技能。

　　有时可以把多个能力倾向测试结合在一起，组成多重能力倾向成套测试，例如计算机编程能力倾向测试包很适合用来评估计算机编程人员和系统分析员。在下面的案例研究中，我们会说明这个测试。

　　您或许会注意到，测试出版人会巧妙地使用**能力**和**能力倾向**这两个词，甚至重叠使用。在实际测试中，这个细微的差别不会造成任何影响。

TESTING FOR SELECTION

APTITUDE TESTS

CASE STUDY: CPAB

An aerospace company was looking internally to promote a project manager from five existing systems analysts. Amongst the measures used for assessment was the **Computer Programmers Aptitude Battery (CPAB)**. They decided to use this measure as a screen to identify a final shortlist of two candidates for further assessment.

The CPAB is ideal for recruiting computer programmers or systems analysts, for assessing both the development needs of existing staff and potential trainees. It consists of five modular timed tests, measuring the following skills and aptitudes:

1. **Verbal Meaning (8 mins)**: tests communication skills and knowledge of vocabulary commonly used in mathematical, business and systems engineering literature.
2. **Reasoning (20 mins)**: tests ability to translate ideas and operations from word problems into mathematical notations.
3. **Letter Series (10 mins)**: tests abstract reasoning ability, finding a pattern in the given series of letters.
4. **Number Ability (6 mins)**: tests ability to quickly estimate reasonable answers to computations.
5. **Diagramming (5 mins)**: tests ability to analyse a problem and order the steps for solution in a logical sequence.

Used with the kind permission of ASE.

Notes

遴选测试

能力倾向测试

案例研究：CPAB

　　一家航空公司要从内部现有的五名系统分析师当中挑出一人，晋升为项目经理。人员评估采用的方法之一是**计算机编程人员能力倾向测试包（CPAB）**。他们决定用这种测试筛选出两名最终候选人，再做进一步评估。

　　CPAB 非常适合用来招聘计算机编程人员或系统分析师，能评估现有员工和未来实习人员的发展需求。它由 5 个计时的模块测试组成，测量以下技能和能力：

　　1.**言语（8 分钟）**：测试沟通能力和数学、商务和系统工程文献中常使用到的词汇知识。
　　2.**推理（20 分钟）**：测试将文字性概念、操作转换成数学符号的能力。
　　3.**字母系列（10 分钟）**：测试抽象推理能力，找出所给出的一系列字母的模式。
　　4.**数字能力（6 分钟）**：测试快速估算出合理的计算结果的能力。
　　5.**图解（5 分钟）**：测试分析问题、按照逻辑顺序给出解决步骤的能力。

　　经 ASE 允许使用。

TESTING FOR SELECTION

APTITUDE TESTS

SCORING SYSTEMS

All psychometric tests use scoring systems so that candidates can be compared with each other. The most common scoring systems are set out below.

Each item that candidates score correctly earns them one point; this is called their raw score. Using tables, these raw scores are converted into:

- **T-score** (transformed score, on a scale of 20-80)
- **Percentile** (score level below which others may have scored)
- **Sten** (score out of 10)
- **Grade** (A-E)

Notes

_____

_____

_____

_____

_____

能力倾向测试

评分系统

所有的心理测试都采用评分系统，能够对不同的应试者进行相互比对。最常用的评分系统如下：

应试者每回答正确一道题目，得一分；这称作他们的原始分。通过表格，把原始分转化为：

- **T分**（转化后的分数，范围为 20-80）

- **百分比**（他人得分比其低的百分比）

- **十分制**（满分 10 分）

- **等级**（A 到 E）

TESTING FOR SELECTION

APTITUDE TESTS
CASE STUDY: CPAB RESULTS

The line manager and HR director were presented with the following data:

Name	Verbal Meaning		Reasoning		Letter Series		Number Ability		Diagramming		Decision
	Sten	%ile	Sten	%ile	Sten	%ile	Sten	%ile	Sten	%ile	
AB	5	42	6	58	5	42	4	22	3	12	Not progressed
CD	9	96	8	92	9	96	7	78	9	96	Shortlisted
EF	6	58	7	78	6	58	5	42	7	78	Not progressed*
GH	3	12	4	22	5	42	3	12	4	22	Not progressed
IJ	7	78	7	78	8	92	8	92	8	92	Shortlisted

*Not progressed (but keep on file with consent)

- Candidate **CD: Sten results are 9, 8, 9, 7, 9 at 96th percentile**
- Candidate **IJ : Sten results are 7, 7, 8, 8, 8, at 92nd percentile**

The candidates also took further assessments, including work performance measures and management reports. After consideration of all the results it was decided that **AB** and **GH** would not progress further on this occasion. **EF** scored just above average and, although not moved on to the management stream, will be considered for future supervisor training.

Used with the kind permission of ASE.

Notes

能力倾向测试

案例研究：CPAB 结果

部门经理和人力资源主管看到的结果如下：

姓名	言语		推理		字母系列		数字能力		图解		结论
	十分制	百分比	十分制	百分比	十分制	百分比	十分制	百分比	十分制	百分比	
AB	5	42	6	58	5	42	4	22	3	12	落选
CD	9	96	8	92	9	96	7	78	9	96	入选
EF	6	58	7	78	6	58	5	42	7	78	落选*
GH	3	12	4	22	5	42	3	12	4	22	落选
IJ	7	78	7	78	8	92	8	92	8	92	入选

* 落选（但同意留档）

候选人 CD：十分制结果分别是 9，8，9，7，9，百分比为 96%

候选人 IJ：十分制结果分别为 7,7,8,8,8，百分比为 92%

对候选人进行了进一步评估，包括工作绩效测试和管理报告。经过对所有结果的考虑，决定是 AB 和 GH 不能入选本次晋升。EF 的分数刚刚到平均值，尽管不能晋级到管理层，但考虑未来对他进行管理层培训。

经 ASE 允许使用。

TESTING FOR SELECTION

CRITICAL REASONING TESTS

We look next at critical reasoning tests.

In today's very fast moving business environment sometimes more general, rather than specific, abilities are required of managers. This is particularly so in the financial sector of a business. Financial directors need not only to understand the precise detail of financial management but also require a broader, more general understanding of the wider business context so that they can match their financial strategies against those of their competitors.

Tests have been designed to look broadly at the wider competence of **critically analysing** situations and data.

The following case study demonstrates how a critical reasoning test can be beneficial in an organisational setting.

Notes

遴选测试

逻辑推理测试

下面我们来看逻辑推理测试。

在如今快速变化的商业环境中，有时候经理需要的是综合性的能力，而不是具体的能力。商业金融领域更是如此。财务主管不仅要了解金融管理的准确细节，也要对整体商业环境有全面、综合的了解，这样才能调整财务战略以便与竞争对手抗衡。

人们设计了专门的测试，针对情景和数据的**逻辑分析**能力进行全面考察。

下面的案例研究向您展示了逻辑推理测试是如何在组织中发挥作用的。

TESTING FOR SELECTION

CRITICAL REASONING TESTS

CASE STUDY: W-GCTA^{UK}

The board of a publishing house marketing a fashion, food and lifestyle weekly are seeking to recruit a new finance director. They are keen to appoint someone with more than just sound financial competence. The fast-moving, dynamic fashion environment demands someone responsive to change and innovation, with a broad understanding of the publishing world but, above all, with the ability critically to appraise the marketplace and competitors' tactics and strategy.

The CEO has employed a headhunter for the search and has heard that the **Watson Glaser Critical Thinking Appraisal (WGCTA)** can identify competencies relevant to the post, including the ability to think critically and appraise business situations rapidly, considered essential for this position.

The W-GCTA was developed by Goodwin Watson (1925) and Edward Glaser (1937), with the intention of combining theoretical aspects of critical thinking with the practical issues of producing measures that could be used in organisational settings. Professor John Rust (2002) has produced the latest UK version referred to as the **W-GCTA^{UK}**.

Notes

_____

_____

_____

_____

_____

遴选测试

逻辑推理测试

案例研究：W–GCTA^{uk}

　　一家出版时尚、美食和生活方式周刊的出版社董事会正在招聘新的财务主管，他们的理想人选不仅要具备扎实的财务能力，还要能够在快速变化、充满活力的时尚界对变化和创新做出迅速反应，对出版业有深入了解，最重要的是要具备逻辑推理能力，能够评估市场和竞争对手的战术策略。

　　总裁聘请了猎头来寻找候选人，并得知**沃森－格拉瑟批判性思维评价表（WGCTA）**能识别与职位相关的能力，包括批判性思维和快速评估商业环境，这两项能力对这个职位非常重要。

　　W–GCTA 是由古德温·沃森（1925）和爱德华·格拉瑟（1937）研发的，目的是把批判性思维的理论和可在组织中使用的实际解决问题的方案结合起来。约翰·拉斯特教授（2002）研发了最新的英国版本，称作 W–GCTA^{uk}。

TESTING FOR SELECTION

CRITICAL REASONING TESTS

HOW THE W-GCTA^UK TEST WORKS

The **W-GCTA^UK** includes problems, statements, arguments and interpretations: processes similar to those encountered on a daily basis in various responsible management roles.

The W-GCTA^UK measures five areas of critical thinking capability, based on an individual's ability to:

1. Make accurate inferences.
2. Recognise assumptions.
3. Evaluate argument.
4. Deduce reasoning.
5. Interpret information logically.

Used with the kind permission of Harcourt Assessment

Notes

_____

_____

_____

_____

_____

遴选测试

逻辑推理测试

W–GCTA^{uk} 测试如何起作用

W–GCTA^{uk} 包括问题、报表、论证和阐释：过程与不同管理角色在日常工作中遇到的情景相似。

基于个人在以下五个方面的能力，W–GCTA^{uk} 测试五个方面的批判思维能力：

1. 做出准确推断
2. 识别假设
3. 评估论证
4. 演绎推理
5. 逻辑解读信息

经哈考特评估测试公司允许使用。

TESTING FOR SELECTION

CRITICAL REASONING TESTS

CASE STUDY: W-GCTA[UK]

The headhunter agrees that the W-GCTA[UK] is an appropriate test for the finance director post in this organisation and sets up a testing session for a shortlist of five candidates.

The Watson-Glaser is an easy-to-administer measure of analytical reasoning skills. Each candidate's task is to read a passage from the question booklet, consider a series of propositions relating to given statements, study each statement and evaluate how appropriate or valid these propositions are.

The CEO has asked the headhunter to supply her with a list of the top three candidates' scores, together with a range of assessment centre exercises including scores from The Rust Advanced Numerical Reasoning Appraisal (RANRA), used to assess numerical critical thinking skills relevant to financial competence.

The results table for W-GCTA[UK] is shown on the next page.

Notes

_____

_____

_____

_____

_____

遴选测试

逻辑推理测试

案例研究：W–GCTA^{uk}

　　猎头赞同 W–GCTA^{uk} 适合用来招聘这个组织的财务主管岗位，因此对五名入围的应聘者制定了测试环节。

　　沃森－格拉瑟测试的是分析推理能力，操作简单。每位应聘者从问题册上读一段内容，思考与给出的论述相关的建议，分析每个论述，并评价这些建议是否合适、有效。

　　按照总裁的要求，猎头给出了排名前三的应聘者结果，还有一系列评估中心的测试，包括拉斯特高级数字推理评估 (RANRA) 得分，用来评估财务相关的数字批判思维能力。

　　W–GCTA^{uk} 的结果列表如下页所示。

经哈考特评估测试公司允许使用。

CRITICAL REASONING TESTS

CASE STUDY: W-GCTA^UK TABLE OF RESULTS

Name	Inference-raw score out of 16	Recognition of assumptions	Deduction	Interpretation	Evaluation of arguments	Total raw score	T-Score	Percentile	Sten	Grade	Decision
AB	10	12	13	15	15	65	59	82	7	B	2nd interview
CD	8	10	11	10	12	51	43	24	4	C	Not called for interview
EF	13	13	13	13	13	65	59	82	7	B	2nd interview

Notes

_____

_____

_____

_____

_____

逻辑推理测试

案例研究：W–GCTA[uk] 结果列表

姓名	推理 — 原始分 总分16	识别假设	推断	解读	评估论证	原始总分	T 分	百分比	十分制	等级	结果
AB	10	12	13	15	15	65	59	82	7	B	第二轮面试
CD	8	10	11	10	12	51	43	24	4	C	无面试资格
EF	13	13	13	13	13	65	59	82	7	B	第二轮面试

TESTING FOR SELECTION

CRITICAL REASONING TESTS

CASE STUDY: W-GCTA^UK CONCLUSION

Looking at each candidate's scores, the CEO observes that **AB** and **EF** have the same **raw score of 65** (actual scores on the test), but the distribution of those scores between tests and between candidates is very different. It looks as if **EF** is more consistent, scoring **13** for each element. The CEO considers this consistency to be a valuable attribute and will invite **AB** and **EF** back for a second interview, after the results of further exercises undertaken in the assessment centre have been analysed.

CD's application will not be taken further.

It is important at this point to remind ourselves that personnel decisions **should not be taken on tests results alone**. This is why the CEO is asking for results from other exercises to be considered.

 *Notes*

遴选测试

逻辑推理测试

案例研究：W−GCTA^{uk} 结论

观察每位应聘者的分数，总裁发现 **AB** 和 **EF** 的**原始分一样，都是 65 分**（测试的实际得分），但他们的得分分布相差很大，EF 的分数更加一致，每个部分都是 13。总裁认为这种一致性很难得，决定在评估中心对其他测试结果进行分析之后，邀请 **AB** 和 **EF** 都进行第二轮面试。

不再考虑 CD 的申请。

需要提醒的一点是，人事决策**不应该仅仅基于测试结果**，这也是为什么总裁要参考其他测试结果的原因。

经哈考特评估测试公司允许使用。

TESTING FOR SELECTION

PERSONALITY TESTS
THE MYTH OF THE PERFECT PERSONALITY

Having looked at aptitude and critical reasoning tests, we now move on to personality tests.

It is important to state that there is no such thing as a perfect personality for any work situation or other context in testing. The 'perfect personality profile' approach (where people believe that there is an ideal profile to fit a job) is a fallacious argument containing several pitfalls:

- Most perfect profiles are derived from people doing the job, taking no account of how **well** they do it

- A perfect profile may show how well people have adapted to the job's demands, not how well people with that profile are naturally comfortable with doing the job

- The perfect profile approach encourages cloning – only selecting as managers people who closely resemble existing managers. This may create great harmony and satisfaction within the organisation, but could make the organisation very vulnerable and too comfortable when faced with the need to change. Diversity of personality is often an advantage, in any organisation

Notes

人格测试

完美人格的神话

看过能力倾向测试和逻辑推理测试，我们现在来看一下人格测试。

需要声明的是，不存在所谓的完美人格，能够适合任何工作背景或测试中的情景，这一点很重要。培养"完美人格特征"（人们认为有符合某项工作的完美特征）是一个谬论，错误在于：

• 大部分的完美特征源于做那项工作的人，而没有考虑他们做得**有多好**。

• 完美特征或许能反映人们有多适应职位要求，而不是具备这种特征的人天生就适合那项工作。

• 培养完美特征是鼓励人们克隆——只是选出与现任经理非常相似的人担任经理，这可能会使内部达到和谐满意，却可能导致组织在面临改变的需求时遭到冲击、过于安逸。在任何组织中，人格的多样化都往往是优势。

TESTING FOR SELECTION

PERSONALITY TESTS

There are hundreds of personality tests available and it is very difficult even for the expert to choose the test that fits all situations; it is a bit like choosing a single pair of shoes to suit all the activities you might do on holiday: walking, playing sport, dancing or going to a smart restaurant.

Instead, when thinking of applying a personality test, we should perhaps ask how a person with a particular personality profile or personality traits is likely to perform in the context we are considering, which is – how the organisation can best meet its development objectives through the greater understanding of an individual's personality.

On the next few pages we illustrate, through a case study in development, a foundation test: the **16 Personality Factor Questionnaire** (16PF®5). Dr Raymond Cattell wrote the 16PF as part of his work to identify the primary components of personality. His research was based on the use of factor analysis to interpret data derived from questionnaire items and from behavioural ratings. This test has an extensive pedigree of research reliability and validity, gathered over the last 60 years, and is of particular use in selection, personal development and change.

Notes

_____

_____

_____

_____

_____

人格测试

现在有成百上千种人格测试，即使专家也很难选出一个适合所有情景的测试；这就像要挑一双适合假日所有活动的鞋子：走路、运动、跳舞或去高级餐厅。

相反，在考虑应用人格测试时，或许该问问具备某种人格特征或个性特质的人在我们所考虑的情景下可能有什么样的表现，即企业如何通过更多地了解个人人格而最好地实现其发展目标。

下面几页我们通过一个发展的案例研究展示一种基础测试：**16种人格因素问卷（16PF®5）**。雷蒙德·卡特尔博士在其著作中编写了 16PF 测试，用来识别人格的主要组成部分。他的研究基于使用因子分析来对问卷题目和行为评估得来的数据进行解读。这项测试收集了 60 多年来的数据，具有研究可靠性和有效性，在选拔人员、个人发展和改变时非常有用。

TESTING FOR SELECTION

PERSONALITY TESTS

CASE STUDY: 16PF PROFILE

A large retailer looking to fill the position of call centre manager by an internal promotion was advised to use the 16PF (5th Edition). Zofia, one of those being considered, came across at work as confident and keen to take on more responsibility.

These traits were supported by her profile (see page 62) which shows a just above average level of confidence (sten 7-socially bold, Factor H) and a preference for taking the lead and being in control (sten 8-dominance, Factor E). The profile also shows less suitable traits. A sten 2 score for emotional stability (Factor C) suggests someone reactive, prone to mood swings and not calm under pressure. This could affect her management of customers and staff, particularly with a low score for warmth (sten 1-warmth, Factor A) and high physical tension (sten 9-tension, Factor Q4) indicating an amount of restless impatience.

Her enthusiastic approach to work is shown by a sten 8 score for liveliness (Factor F) but a high score for vigilance (sten 10-vigilance, Factor L) suggests she may be suspicious of other people's views and motives, leading her to reject their opinions and ideas in an inflexible way. Her tolerance for disorder and leaving things to chance (sten 3-perfectionism, Factor Q3) may impede her ability to drive for results and motivate others.

Notes

人格测试

案例研究：16PF 人格测试

一家大型零售商在内部寻找呼叫中心经理候选人，他们被建议使用 16PF（第五版）。 苏菲亚是其中一个考虑人选，她在工作中充满自信，愿意承担更多责任。

她的特征描述（见 63 页）反映了她自信心略高于平均值（7/10——敢于与人交际，因素 H），有领导力和控制力倾向（8/10——控制力，因素 E）。同时反映出一些不太适合的特点，情绪稳定一项的得分是 2/10（因素 C），说明反应激烈，情绪易波动，压力下不能保持冷静，这会影响她管理客户和员工，尤其是亲和力得分较低（1/10——亲和力，因素 A），生理紧张得分较高（9/10——紧张，因素 Q4），说明有一定程度的焦虑和急躁。

她活力（因素 F）得分 8/10，说明对工作有热情，但是警惕性（10/10——警惕性，因素 L）分值很高，说明对他人的观点和动机有疑心，会导致她生硬地拒绝别人的意见和想法。对于混乱的忍受和顺其自然（3/10——完美主义，因素 Q3）可能会遏制她实现目标的动力和激励他人的能力。

TESTING FOR SELECTION
PERSONALITY TESTS

CASE STUDY: 16PF PROFILE

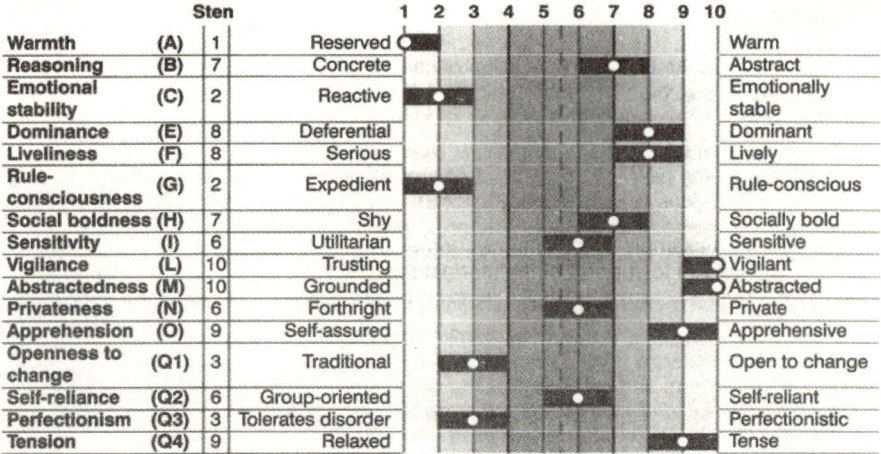

		Sten	Low pole	Sten 1 2 3 4 5 6 7 8 9 10	High pole
Warmth	(A)	1	Reserved	○ (1)	Warm
Reasoning	(B)	7	Concrete	(7)	Abstract
Emotional stability	(C)	2	Reactive	(2)	Emotionally stable
Dominance	(E)	8	Deferential	(8)	Dominant
Liveliness	(F)	8	Serious	(8)	Lively
Rule-consciousness	(G)	2	Expedient	(2)	Rule-conscious
Social boldness	(H)	7	Shy	(7)	Socially bold
Sensitivity	(I)	6	Utilitarian	(6)	Sensitive
Vigilance	(L)	10	Trusting	(10) ○	Vigilant
Abstractedness	(M)	10	Grounded	(10) ○	Abstracted
Privateness	(N)	6	Forthright	(6)	Private
Apprehension	(O)	9	Self-assured	(9)	Apprehensive
Openness to change	(Q1)	3	Traditional	(3)	Open to change
Self-reliance	(Q2)	6	Group-oriented	(6)	Self-reliant
Perfectionism	(Q3)	3	Tolerates disorder	(3)	Perfectionistic
Tension	(Q4)	9	Relaxed	(9)	Tense

Notes

_____

_____

_____

_____

_____

遴选测试

人格测试

案例研究：16PF 人格测试

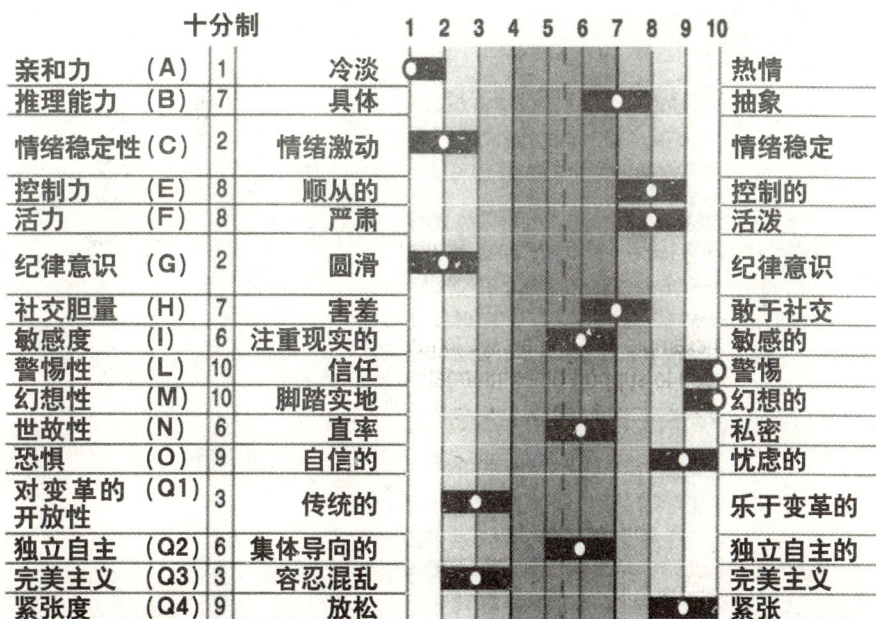

十分制				1	2	3	4	5	6	7	8	9	10		
亲和力	(A)	1	冷淡												热情
推理能力	(B)	7	具体												抽象
情绪稳定性	(C)	2	情绪激动												情绪稳定
控制力	(E)	8	顺从的												控制的
活力	(F)	8	严肃												活泼
纪律意识	(G)	2	圆滑												纪律意识
社交胆量	(H)	7	害羞												敢于社交
敏感度	(I)	6	注重现实的												敏感的
警惕性	(L)	10	信任												警惕
幻想性	(M)	10	脚踏实地												幻想的
世故性	(N)	6	直率												私密
恐惧	(O)	9	自信的												忧虑的
对变革的开放性	(Q1)	3	传统的												乐于变革的
独立自主	(Q2)	6	集体导向的												独立自主的
完美主义	(Q3)	3	容忍混乱												完美主义
紧张度	(Q4)	9	放松												紧张

PERSONALITY TESTS
CASE STUDY: 16PF CONCLUSION

The HR director, in consultation with the managing director, decided not to promote Zofia but, in order to maintain her motivation and utilise her outstanding product knowledge, she was offered external coaching.

This 16PF profile, used in conjunction with discussions with Zofia, and other evidence of how she related to her colleagues, helped Zofia's manager take an appropriate and agreed set of decisions, which worked to Zofia's advantage.

Here then is an example of using a psychometric test which presents a rather negative picture of a person to support other information, like workplace reports and interviews, to make personnel decisions **to the advantage of the organisation and the candidate.**

Notes

_____

_____

_____

_____

遴选测试

人格测试

案例研究：16PF 结论

人力资源主管和总经理讨论后，决定不晋升苏菲亚，但为了让她保持动力，发挥她出众的产品知识，给她提供了外部教练的机会。

苏菲亚的经理使用 16PF 测试，并参考了与苏菲亚的讨论及苏菲亚和同事互动的证明材料，做出了合适、令人满意的决定，从而发挥了苏菲亚的优势。

这个例子是利用心理测试反映个人的负面形象，来支持工作场所报告和面试等其他信息，使企业做出**有利于企业和应聘者**的人事决策。

PERSONALITY TESTS

PERSONALITY OR BEHAVIOUR

Personality traits can be reliably tested by most valid and reliable instruments. Research shows that these traits do not transfer absolutely into behaviour in the workplace. This is because the workplace environment will cause some change of the pure personality trait into the accepted workplace culture of an organisation. Workplace behaviour can be modified by the situation; tests can help indicate possible directions for such modification.

Some instruments, because they are designed to pick up these working style behaviours, are particularly appropriate to use in measuring the way that people may use their personality to form their own particular management style. This will be demonstrated in the next psychometric instrument, the **Personal Profile Analysis**, and accompanying **Human Job Analysis**. These instruments offer useful insights into work style behaviours demanded of a particular job function.

Notes

_____

_____

_____

_____

_____

人格测试

人格还是行为

人格特征可以通过大多数有效和可靠的工具测量出来。研究表明，这些特征并不一定都会转换为职场行为，因为职场环境会导致一些纯粹的人格特征转变为被某个组织接受的职场文化。职场行为随环境而变化；而测试有助于指明这种变化可能的方向。

专门有一些工具是用来识别这些职场行为方式的，因此尤其适用于测试人们如何利用人格形成自己独特的管理方式。下面的心理测试工具，即**个人形象分析**和伴随的人类**工作分析**能说明这一点。这些测量工具为某个具体岗位需要的工作行为方式提供了有用的观察视角。

TESTING FOR SELECTION

WORK STYLE TESTS

CASE STUDY: THOMAS INTERNATIONAL SYSTEM PPA

An organisation that specialises in selling off-plan properties around the globe, from Spain to the Caribbean, is looking to recruit a sales person to work in their international office in Spain. The ability to speak Spanish will be an important attribute in the selection process in order to understand local property processes adequately and communicate fluently in both English and Spanish.

Three Spanish speakers have been short-listed and asked to complete a work style inventory, following the Thomas International System.

Notes

遴选测试

工作风格测试

案例研究：托马斯国际体系PPA

　　一家在世界范围内（从西班牙到加勒比海区域）从事期房销售的组织，目前正在为西班牙的国际办公室招聘销售人员。为了充分了解当地房产处理流程，能流利地使用英语和西班牙语进行沟通，会说西班牙语是挑选时的一个重要特质。

　　已经有三名会讲西班牙语的人入围，他们要完成一份遵循托马斯国际系统的工作风格量表。

TESTING FOR SELECTION

WORK STYLE TESTS

HOW THE THOMAS SYSTEM PPA WORKS

The work style inventory selected was the **Thomas International Personal Profile Analysis (PPA)**. The PPA is designed around the DISC model of workplace behaviour. The history of the DISC models of assessment is grounded in the psychological theory of sensing, intuition, thinking and feeling developed in the 1920s by Carl G Jung in his book *The Psychological Types*. It was in 1928 that William Moulton Marston highlighted in his book, *Emotions of Normal People* the types **D** = Dominance, **I** = Inducement, **S** = Submission and **C** = Compliance (DISC) as types of behavioural response to a perceived friendly or hostile environment.

The types and trait words that have been interpreted by Thomas International are:

		HIGH	LOW
D	Dominance	driving, competitive, direct	modest, peaceful, unassuming
I	Influence	optimistic, self-promoting	reserved, reflective, retiring
S	Steadiness	dependable, self-controlled, easy-going	impatient, mobile, active
C	Compliance	disciplined, perfection-seeking, logical	firm, obstinate, persistent

Some material copyright Thomas International Ltd, reproduced here with their permission.

Notes

工作风格测试

托马斯系统 PPA 如何发挥作用

选用的工作风格量表是**托马斯国际个体行为特征分析（PPA）**，根据职场行为的 DISC 模型设计而成。DISC 评估模型基于感觉、直觉、思考和感受的心理理论，这个心理理论是 20 世纪 20 年代卡尔·荣格在其《心理类型》一书中提出的。1928 年，威廉·莫尔森·马斯顿在他的著作《正常人的情感》中强调：D 型 = 支配型，I 型 = 影响型，S 型 = 稳健型，C 型 = 服从型（DISC），这些类型是对感知到的友好或敌意的环境所产生的行为反应。

托马斯国际用来阐释类型和特质的词语有：

		高	低
D	支配型	精力旺盛，好竞争，直接	谦逊，平和，不爱出风头
I	影响型	乐观，自我促进	内敛，反省，不善社交
S	稳健型	可信赖，自我约束，易相处	急躁，适应性强，积极
C	服从型	守纪律，追求完美，有逻辑	坚定，顽固，执着

部分材料版权归托马斯国际所有，经同意后转载。

TESTING FOR SELECTION

WORK STYLE TESTS

CASE STUDY: THOMAS SYSTEM PPA

The Thomas System PPA comprises three main assessments: the Human Job Analysis (HJA), which analyses a job in terms of DISC; the Personal Profile Analysis (PPA), measuring the personal attributes of a candidate; and finally Ability Tests for Selection and Training (which we do not go into here).

The company selected this particular inventory because the combination of Personal Profile Analysis and Human Job Analysis, completed by the organisation and outlining the necessary job requirements involved in selling off-plan properties, is a compact model looking at both job and person in the same terms.

The requirements revealed by the HJA for this position are:

- Strong influencing skills
- Assertiveness
- Fast pace of operation in a dynamic environment

Notes

遴选测试

工作风格测试

案例研究：托马斯系统 PPA

　　托马斯系统 PPA 主要由三个评估组成：职位分析（HJA），即从 DISC 角度分析某个职位；行为特征分析（PPA），测试候选人的个性特质；选拔与培训能力测试（这里不作深入解释）。

　　公司选择这个量表是因为它把行为特征分析和由组织完成的职位分析结合起来，再加上期房销售必需的岗位要求，就能形成一个精简模型，可以以同样的标准考察岗位和人员。

　　HJA 显示的岗位要求是：

- 较强的影响力
- 果敢自信
- 动态环境中的快速执行力

部分材料版权归托马斯国际所有，经同意后转载。

TESTING FOR SELECTION

WORK STYLE TESTS

THOMAS SYSTEM PPA

The Thomas System PPA provides insight into workplace behaviour looking at:

- Strengths and limitations – current job performance in terms of behavioural preferences in a work context
- Ability to self-start – get up and go without prompting
- Communication style – how a manager may interact with others with respect to their preferred behavioural style
- Motivation – motivational patterns as derived from workplace preferences

Notes

工作风格测试

托马斯系统 PPA

托马斯系统 PPA 能为职场行为提供洞见，它关注的是：

- 优势和局限——工作环境中，就行为偏好而言，现在的工作表现
- 自主能力——不需要催促就能行动
- 沟通方式——经理如何以对方偏好的行为方式与他人互动
- 动机——来自职场偏好的激励方式

部分材料版权归托马斯国际所有，经同意后转载。

TESTING FOR SELECTION

WORK STYLE TESTS

THOMAS SYSTEM PPA PROCEDURE

The PPA provides a profile measuring the key behavioural characteristics or workplace style of an individual at work. A series of 24 questions on a forced choice, ipsative (self-referential), 'first impressions' basis, outlines candidates' styles on four main dimensions: Dominance, Influence, Steadiness and Compliance (DISC).

When used for selection, the PPA should be preceded by the Human Job Analysis (HJA) which first identifies the behavioural requirements of a job. Like the PPA, the results are plotted on a graph which provides an objective view of a particular role and indicates the behavioural style of the person most likely to succeed. The PPA profile is then compared with the HJA to look at how well the two profiles fit.

Notes

工作风格测试

托马斯系统 PPA 步骤

PPA 能测试个人工作时的主要行为特征或职场风格，包含 24 个问题，基于强迫选择、自比（自我参考）和"第一印象"，勾勒出应聘者四个主要维度的特征：支配、影响、稳健和服从（DISC）。

在用 PPA 选拔人员时，应该先使用岗位分析（HJA），确定某项工作的行为要求。像 PPA 一样，结果是呈现在表格中的，展示对某个特定角色的客观评判并指出最有可能取得成功的个人行为方式。再把 PPA 结果同 HJA 相比较，观察两个描述的相匹配程度。

部分材料版权归托马斯国际所有，经同意后转载。

TESTING FOR SELECTION

WORK STYLE TESTS

CASE STUDY: THOMAS SYSTEM PPA

The time share company asks three people who know the job well to draw up a job analysis in the profile form of the **Human Job Analysis (HJA)**. The results are plotted on a graph, see next page. Then two short-listed candidates are profiled using the **PPA**, see second and third graphs. Finally, the candidates will be interviewed.

In the HJA profile for the job, the work style of the sales person demands a high level (above centre line) of Dominance and Influence and a lower level (below centre line) of Steadiness and Compliance.

The initial interview with each candidate will be structured to confirm (or deny) their PPA findings and then confirm whether or not the candidate at interview behaves according to their profile or modifies their behaviour (impression management) to influence the interviewers, very common in high stakes situations like recruitment.

The profile graph shows that Candidate 1 fits the HJA most closely. This was confirmed by the structured interview, and he will proceed to the next stage. Candidate 2 reports himself as fitting the job in only two of the scales, so may not feel comfortable in the role.

Some material copyright Thomas International Ltd, reproduced here with their permission.

Notes

_____

_____

_____

_____

_____

遴选测试

工作风格测试

案例研究：托马斯系统PPA

　　分时公司请了三名非常了解此项工作的人在**岗位分析（HJA）**特征表中作岗位分析，将结果标示在表格中，见下页。再使用**PPA**评价两名初步审核通过的应聘者，如第二和第三个表所示。最后，对两位应聘者进行面试。

　　在HJA的工作描述中，销售人员的工作方式需要较高的（高于中间值）支配性和影响力，较低的（低于中间值）稳健性和服从性。

　　每位应聘者的初试是为了确认（或否定）他们的PPA结果，然后弄清楚应聘者在面试中的行为是否与他们的描述吻合，还是他们为了影响面试官，行为发生了改变（印象管理），这在招聘这样的高利益相关的情景中很常见。

　　特征图表明，1号应聘者最符合HJA，结构化面试也确认了这一点，他将进入到下一轮。2号应聘者只有两个量度适合这项工作，有可能会不适应这个角色。

部分材料版权归托马斯国际所有，经同意后转载。

TESTING FOR SELECTION

WORK STYLE INVENTORY

CASE STUDY: THOMAS SYSTEM PPA PROFILES

Human Job Analysis Graph

D I S C

12
11
10
9
8
7
6
5
4
3
2
1
0
-1
-2
-3
-4
-5
-6
-7
-8
-9
-10
-11
-12

High D & I
Low S & C

Candidate 1 Graph

D I S C

High D & I
Low S & C
Fit organisation is looking for

Candidate 2 Graph

D I S C

High I & S
Low D & C
Poor fit

Some material copyright Thomas International Ltd, reproduced here with their permission.

Notes

遴选测试

工作风格量表

案例研究：托马斯系统 PPA 特征

岗位分析表

DISC

12
11
10
9
8
7
6
5
4
3
2
1
0
-1
-2
-3
-4
-5
-6
-7
-8
-9
-10
-11
-12

高 D&I
低 S&C

1 号应聘者

DISC

高 D&I
低 S&C
符合企业人选

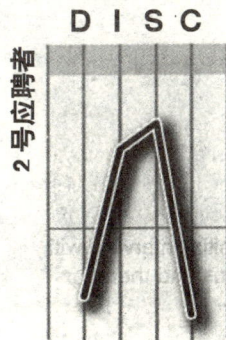

2 号应聘者

DISC

高 I&S
低 D&C
很不符合

部分材料版权归托马斯国际所有，经同意后转载。

— 81 —

TESTING FOR SELECTION

WORK STYLE INVENTORY

CASE STUDY: THOMAS SYSTEM PPA CONCLUSION

The Thomas System is designed to fit 'round pegs into round holes'. It helps us understand that if we can outline the behavioural aspects of a job and then fill that position with a candidate whose behavioural style closely matches the requirements of that job then job satisfaction, retention, productivity and the bottom line should all be improved.

Notes

_____

_____

_____

_____

_____

工作风格量表

案例研究：托马斯系统 PPA 结论

托马斯系统的目的是使每个人"各得其所"，它帮助我们认识到如果给出某个岗位的行为描述，再寻找行为风格匹配工作要求的应聘者填补这个岗位，就能提高工作满意度、人员保持率、生产效率和盈利状况。

TESTING FOR ORGANISATIONAL DEVELOPMENT

组织发展测试

TESTING FOR ORGANISATIONAL DEVELOPMENT

WHAT IS ORGANISATIONAL DEVELOPMENT?

Organisational development (OD) has been defined as *'the process of planned change, learning and development, and improvement in the organisation through the application of knowledge of behavioural sciences'*. (Moorhead & Griffin, Organisational behaviour: managing people and organisations)

In simple terms, it means that the application of psychometric tests can help to improve the performance of individuals, teams and the organisation as a whole because tests can measure, as part of the process, **the potential for performance**.

In today's changing and volatile world, organisations are continually looking for ways to improve performance and satisfy the demands of their customers, clients and other key stakeholders. For an organisation to evolve, the people working within it will have to adapt; and for this to be successful, they first of all need to know what it is about the way they are currently performing that needs to change.

We next describe a case study using emotional intelligence (EI) in OD.

Notes

_____

_____

_____

_____

_____

组织发展测试

什么是组织发展?

组织发展 (OD) 的定义是"通过应用行为科学的知识,在组织中进行有计划的变革、学习和发展,以及提高的过程"。(摩海德 & 格里芬,《组织行为学:组织与人员的管理》)。

简单来说,就是运用心理测试能够帮助提升个人、团队和组织整体的绩效,因为作为其中一个环节,测试能测量出**绩效潜能**。

在当今充满变化和动荡的世界,组织在不断寻找提高绩效的途径,以期满足顾客、客户和其他利益相关者的要求。组织要想发展,组织内部的人就必须适应;要想顺利适应,首先得知道现在的哪些行为是需要改变的。

接下来看一个在组织发展中运用情商 (EI) 的案例研究。

TESTING FOR ORGANISATIONAL DEVELOPMENT

WHAT IS EMOTIONAL INTELLIGENCE (EI)?

EI is about the ability to understand oneself and express feelings, to understand how others feel and be able to relate to them, and to change and manage emotional behaviours in a positive way.

The words 'emotional intelligence' were first used by B. Leuner in 1966, nearly a quarter of a century before Peter Salovey and John Mayer's first article appeared on the topic in 1990. Salovey and Mayer are both highly regarded psychologists still active in the field of EI. It is, however, Daniel Goleman, author of *'Emotional Intelligence'* (1995), and *'Working with Emotional Intelligence'* (1998) who has played the most critical role in the creation of the opportunities for the EI field.

Goleman writes and talks about emotional intelligence in ways that receive the attention of people outside the field of psychology and he has put EI onto the world map. From being a taboo topic in the business arena, emotions are now mentioned in workplace settings. To quote Daniel Goleman, 'The rules for work are changing and being judged by a new yardstick, not just how smart we are, or our expertise, but also how well we handle ourselves and each other'.

Notes

什么是情商（EI）？

　　EI 是了解自我、表达感受，理解他人感受并能够与他们相处，以积极的方式改变、管理情感行为的能力。

　　"情商"这个词最先由 B. 柳纳在 1966 年提出，比彼得·萨洛维和约翰·梅耶在 1990 年首篇谈论这个话题的文章早了近四分之一个世纪。萨洛维和梅耶都是颇负声望的心理学家，至今仍活跃在 EI 领域。但是，《情商》和《情商 3：影响你一生的工作情商》的作者丹尼尔·戈尔曼是 EI 领域最重要的人物，极大地拓展了 EI 领域。

　　戈尔曼书中谈论情商的方式引起了心理学领域以外的人的注意，并让人们记住了 EI 这个词。情绪以前是商业领域的禁忌话题，现在常在工作情景中提到。引用丹尼尔·戈尔曼的话，"工作规则在不断变化，不断有新的衡量标准出现，不仅要看我们有多聪明或专业知识怎样，还要看我们对自己和他人的管理状况如何。"

USING EI TESTS FOR ORGANISATIONAL DEVELOPMENT

Organisations facing 21st century challenges of globalisation, downsizing, merging or restructuring, require their people to be more accountable and more visible within the organisation. These new challenges demand new personal qualities such as taking the initiative, empathy, adaptability and teamwork.

The notion that EI matters at work is now very compelling. We all have seen situations in the workplace where emotions and feelings have had a very real impact on the quality of interactions, relationships and behaviours, affecting the performance of the organisation as a whole. A phrase often heard: 'people don't leave jobs, they leave managers' perhaps emphasises the importance of an understanding of EI.

Notes

_____

_____

_____

_____

_____

组织发展测试

利用情商测试来实现组织发展

面对 21 世纪全球化、裁员、兼并和重组的挑战，组织有可能需要组织内部的员工承担更多责任。这些新的挑战需要新的个人素质，如主动性、同理心、适应性和团队合作。

情商在工作中起着至关重要的作用，这一点毋庸置疑。我们都见识过工作场合中情绪和感受对互动、关系和行为产生的切实冲击，这些影响了组织整体的绩效。有句话常常听到："员工离开的不是公司，而是管理者"，或许强调的就是了解情商的重要性。

TESTING FOR ORGANISATIONAL DEVELOPMENT

EMOTIONAL INTELLIGENCE

CASE STUDY: BAR-ON EQ-I

A large banking organisation was looking for a team leader to promote within their IT department. The candidate selected for the job seemed an ideal choice. Matteo had left university with a first class degree in Computing, followed by a Masters degree in Systems Analysis. He was, without doubt, very bright and focused on his job and quickly gathered expertise at systems problem solving. Matteo accepted the promotion and became team leader of a group of 10 people. He had never actually managed people before, only a square box in front of him, which did not answer back!

Matteo's lack of people skills soon created tensions within the team. HR, after consultation with his manager, decided to refer him to an executive coach. The coach wanted to help Matteo understand himself better as a way to nurture his people skills and manage more positively his social interactions with his team. It was decided to administer the **Bar-On Emotional Quotient Inventory (EQ-i)**, developed by Dr Reuven Bar-On. The EQ-i is a measure of emotionally and socially intelligent behaviour **which provides an estimate of one's underlying emotional-social intelligence.**

Notes

_____

_____

_____

_____

_____

组织发展测试

情商

案例研究：Bar-on EQ-i

　　一家大型银行在 IT 部门物色提拔一名团队领导，选出的候选人看上去很理想。马泰奥大学毕业，拥有计算机学士学位和系统分析硕士学位。毫无疑问，他聪明，专注于工作并迅速掌握了解决系统问题方面的专业知识。升职后，马泰奥成为了 10 个人的团队领导，以前他从未管理过团队，面对的只有一个不会回应的方形盒子！

　　马泰奥缺少人际技能，这很快引起了团队内部的紧张。人力资源经理和他的经理商谈后，决定把他推荐给一位高管教练。教练希望能帮助户马泰奥更多地了解自己，培养人际技能，与队员更积极地进行社交互动。同时决定使用由鲁文·巴昂博士编写的 **Bar-on 情商量表 (EQ-i)**，EQ-i 测试的是情绪智力行为和社交智力行为，**提供对个人潜在情绪－社交智力的评估。**

TESTING FOR ORGANISATIONAL DEVELOPMENT

EMOTIONAL INTELLIGENCE
CASE STUDY: BAR-ON EQ-I

Dr Reuven Bar-On began his work in the field of EI in the 1980s. He was perplexed by a number of questions:

- Why do some people possess greater well-being?
- Why are some people better able to achieve success in life?
- Why do some people who may be blessed with superior intelligence abilities seem to do less well in life, while others with lower intelligence succeed? *S. Stein & H Book: 2001, 2006*

Dr Bar-On originally suggested that effective emotional and social functioning has a positive impact on performance at home, school and in the workplace; and he later developed a number of psychometric instruments to examine this idea.

Returning to the case study, Matteo may have been so focused on studying for his exams that the emotional and social functioning side of his personality was under-developed.

On the following page are the 5 composite scales and 15 subscales which the EQ-i measured when Matteo took the test.

Notes

_____

_____

_____

_____

_____

组织发展测试

情商

案例研究：Bar-on EQ-i

鲁文·巴昂博士从 20 世纪 80 年代开始研究这个领域，当时他对一些问题很困惑：

- 为什么一些人拥有更多的幸福感？
- 为什么一些人生活中更能取得成功？
- 为什么一些人智商很高，生活中却表现得不好，而智商低的人反而取得了成功？（S. 斯坦 & H 布克：2001，2006）

巴昂博士最先提出有效的情绪功能和社交功能对家庭、学校和职场的表现有积极影响，他后来开发了很多心理测量工具检验这个想法。

回到案例研究，马泰奥或许太专注于自己的专业考试，导致人格中的情绪和社交功能没有得到良好发展。

下一页是马泰奥进行EQ-i测试时的 5 个复合量表和 15 个量度。

TESTING FOR ORGANISATIONAL DEVELOPMENT

EMOTIONAL INTELLIGENCE

BAR-ON EQ-I

The instrument is composed of the five scales below that measure the following EI factors, competencies and skills:

- **Intrapersonal** measures the inner self – emotional self-awareness, independence, assertiveness, self-regard and self-actualisation
- **Interpersonal** measures relationship skills – empathy, interpersonal skills and social responsibility
- **Adaptability** measures how we assess and respond to situations – flexibility, reality testing and problem solving
- **Stress management** measures the ability to handle stressful situations without falling apart – stress tolerance and impulse control
- **General mood** measures our outlook on life – self-motivation, optimism and happiness

Used with the kind permission of MHS Multi-Health Systems Inc.

Notes

组织发展测试

情商

Bar-on EQ-i

测量表由下面 5 个量度组成，测量的是 EI 因素、能力和技能：

· **个人内部部分**测量内在的自我——情绪的自我意识、独立性、自信、自尊和自我实现

· **人际部分**测量人际能力——同理心、人际关系和社会责任

· **适应性部分**测量我们如何评估情境并对其做出反应——灵活性、现实验证和解决问题

· **压力管理部分**测量处理压力情境而不崩溃的能力——压力耐受性和冲动控制

· **一般心境部分**测量人生观——自我激励、乐观主义和幸福感

经 MHS 多重健康系统公司许可使用。

EMOTIONAL INTELLIGENCE
CASE STUDY: BAR-ON EQ-I

Matteo completed the EQ-i online using a confidential login and password. The 133 responses to the questionnaire were scored and a fully interpretative user-friendly report was printed in readiness for face-to-face feedback of the results.

Matteo's responses to the questionnaire, examined during the feedback session with his coach, indicated how the various aspects of his emotional intelligence impacted on his behaviour at work. The test results revealed the difficulties he was experiencing when dealing with people and managing stressful situations. His inability to control his temper made his team feel very negative towards him.

Used with the kind permission of MHS Multi-Health Systems Inc.

Notes

_____

_____

_____

_____

_____

组织发展测试

情商

案例研究：Bar-on EQ-i

马泰奥用保密的用户名和密码完成了在线 EQ-i 测试。通过对其问卷的 133 个回答进行评分，打印生成了一份解释透彻、简单易懂的报告，准备进行面对面反馈。

马泰奥的问卷答案，经过教练在反馈环节进行验证，反映了他情商的各个方面对其在工作中行为的影响，结果显示他不能很好地与人相处和处理压力情景。由于不善于控制脾气，团队成员对他的印象很差。

经 MHS 多重健康系统公司许可使用。

TESTING FOR ORGANISATIONAL DEVELOPMENT

EMOTIONAL INTELLIGENCE
CASE STUDY: BAR-ON EQ-I

In discussion with the coach it was decided to work on the following areas of Matteo's emotional intelligence:

- Social awareness and training in interpersonal skills
- Strategies to better manage the emotions of his work colleagues
- Understanding that people as individuals are all different
- Greater flexibility and responsibility in his social interactions
- Improved emotional control to minimise or remove emotional outbursts

As part of the psychometric testing evaluation process, the EQ-i should be administered again after six months to see if there has actually been a change in Matteo's emotional intelligence. A 360 degree feedback assessment is an effective method for understanding workplace performance and will be used for this evaluation.

Used with the kind permission of MHS Multi-Health Systems Inc.

Notes

组织发展测试

情商

案例研究：Bar—on EQ—i

和教练讨论后，决定针对马泰奥情商的以下方面进行改善：

- 社交意识和人际交往能力的培训
- 更好地管理同事情绪的策略
- 认识每个人都是不同的个体
- 增加社交互动中的灵活性和责任感
- 增强情绪控制力，最大限度地减少或消除情绪爆发

作为心理测试评估过程的一部分，EQ—i 应在 6 个月后再进行一次，观察马泰奥的情商是否有变化。360 度反馈评估是了解职场绩效的有效方法，将被用来进行这项评估。

经 MHS 多重健康系统公司许可使用。

TESTING FOR ORGANISATIONAL DEVELOPMENT

EMOTIONAL INTELLIGENCE
MULTI-RATER 360 EI FEEDBACK

Multi-rater 360 EI feedback is a process whereby an individual (the recipient) is rated on his or her emotional intelligence by people (the raters) who know the person, their work and behaviour. Raters can include direct reports, peers and managers and, in some cases, customers or clients. In fact, anybody who is credible to the individual and is familiar with their work can be included in the feedback process.

For an organisation to evolve, the people working within it, such as Matteo, need to adapt to the changes going on around them.

For Matteo to succeed in adapting, he needs to know what it is about his management style that needs to change. He has now found this out and a developmental action plan for behaviour change has been drawn up for him. Six months after administering the EQ-i is an appropriate time to re-evaluate, to see if a change has actually taken place in his emotional intelligence.

The aim of the resulting information is to indicate to the recipient how he is perceived by others.

Used with the kind permission of MHS Multi-Health Systems Inc.

Notes

_____

_____

_____

_____

_____

组织发展测试

情商

360 度情商反馈

360 度情商反馈是个人（即测试对象）由认识他们、了解他们工作和行为的人（评价者）对其情商进行评价。评价者包括直接下属、同僚和经理，有时候还有顾客或客户。实际上，任何值得个人信赖的人和熟悉他们工作的人都能被纳入反馈过程。

组织要发展，在里面工作的人如马泰奥，就需要适应周围不断出现的变化。

马泰奥要想顺利适应变化，就要知道他的哪些管理方式需要改变。现在他找到了需要改变的地方，也制定了针对行为改变的发展计划。EQ-i 测试之后 6 个月是再次评估的最佳时间，观察他的情商是否有改变。

测试结果旨在说明他人是如何评价测试对象的。

经 MHS 多重健康系统公司许可使用。

TESTING FOR ORGANISATIONAL DEVELOPMENT

EMOTIONAL INTELLIGENCE
EQ-360

The EQ-360, a multi-rater tool designed to assess emotional intelligence, was developed by Reuven Bar-On and Richard Handley. It was selected to evaluate Matteo because it fully complements the EQ-i measure of social and emotional intelligence, in that the questions Matteo had been asked when he originally completed the EQ-i were now being asked of his peers, managers, direct reports and other appropriate raters.

In order to identify any specific changes in emotionally and socially intelligent behaviour, and to see if there is congruency between Matteo and his raters, he completes the EQ-i again. All responses are confidential and it is important to make sure that there is a fair share of raters for each category of peers, managers and direct reports.

Matteo's EQ-i scores were noticeably congruent with his raters' scoring in the areas of enhanced interpersonal skills and impulse control. With training, Matteo had been made aware of how emotional and social intelligence could help him manage and lead his team more effectively.

Notes

_____

_____

_____

_____

_____

组织发展测试

情商

EQ-360

EQ-360 是专门用来评估情商的多视角工具，由鲁文·巴昂和理查德·汉德利研发。选择它来评价马泰奥是因为它能充分补充EQ-i 对情绪智力和社交智力的测试。马泰奥之前在EQ-i 中被问到的问题，现在被用来问他的同事、经理、直线上级和其他相关评价者。

为了识别出情绪和社交智力行为上的任何具体变化，观察马泰奥和评价者的反馈是否一致，马泰奥再次进行了 EQ-i 测试。所有回答均保密，同时确保同事、经理和直线上级等评价者的比例合理。

在人际技巧提升和冲动控制两方面，马泰奥的EQ-i 得分与他的评价者给出的分数非常一致。经过培训，马泰奥已经意识到情绪智力和社交智力能帮助他更有效地管理和带领团队。

TESTING FOR ORGANISATIONAL DEVELOPMENT

EMOTIONAL INTELLIGENCE
EQ-360

OTHER BENEFITS TO THE ORGANISATION

Professionally managed, EQ 360 feedback increases individual
self-awareness, and as part of a strategic organisational
process can promote:

- Increased understanding of the behaviours required to
  improve both individual and organisational effectiveness
- More focused development activities, built around the skills
  and competencies required for successful organisational
  performance
- Increased involvement of people at all levels of the organisation
- Increased individual ownership for self-development
  and learning
- Increased familiarity with the implications of robust
  feedback on self-performance in the workplace

Used with the kind permission of MHS Multi-Health Systems Inc.

Notes

_____

_____

_____

_____

_____

组织发展测试

情绪智力

EQ-360

对组织的其他益处

通过专业性的使用，EQ 360 反馈能有效提升个人的自我意识。作为战略组织过程的一部分，它能够促进：

- 对改善个人和组织有效性所需要的行为的理解
- 围绕成功的组织绩效所需要的技能和能力而开展的目标明确的发展活动
- 组织各阶层人员的参与感
- 个人对自我发展和学习的自主性
- 对职场上自我表现反馈的涵义的熟悉程度

经 MHS 多重健康系统公司许可使用。

TESTING FOR ORGANISATIONAL DEVELOPMENT

WELL-BEING & QUALITY OF WORKING LIFE

We are now going to review an OD test which looks at an employee's quality of life.

While financial rewards remain an important source of motivation to some employees, this form of external motivation alone is not enough. Employees have higher expectations of what they want from their employment and are increasingly likely to change companies (and even countries) in search of job satisfaction as part of that elusive quality of life.

In excess of half a million people in the UK at any one time experience stress at levels that make them ill.

Organisations now need to show they are seriously commited to the welfare of their employees, by providing good working conditions leading to a high quality of working life. Our case study illustrates a test that not only helps organisations to attract staff, but also helps to retain existing staff by measuring perceptions on the quality of life in that organisation.

Notes

_____

_____

_____

_____

_____

组织发展测试

幸福感 & 工作生活质量

下面来看一个针对员工生活质量的组织发展测试。

对于一些员工来说，金钱报酬依然是一个重要的激励来源，但只有这种形式的外在动机是不够的。员工对职业有更高的期望，越来越多的员工为了寻求工作满足感和生活质量而换公司（甚至国家）。

英国有超过 50 万人曾承受过足以致病的压力。

如今组织需要表现出对员工福利的切实关怀，提供良好的工作条件和优质的工作生活。这里的案例研究向您展示了一个测试，不仅能帮助组织吸引员工，也能通过测量组织内部对生活质量的感受而留住现有员工。

TESTING FOR ORGANISATIONAL DEVELOPMENT

WELL-BEING

CASE STUDY: QUALITY OF WORKING LIFE QUESTIONNAIRE

The HR manager for a city company raised concern about employee welfare. A yearly staff attendance check had highlighted a higher than expected level of time off work. Analysis of the reasons given revealed high levels of stress, anxiety and other illness, with comments made about the quality of working life in the organisation.

An urgent meeting was held, and the decision taken to undertake an organisational audit to assess the health and well-being climate. The questionnaire selected was the **Quality of Working Life Questionnaire**. It can be used in the following ways at the following levels:

- Across an organisation
- With smaller groups of employees
- When working with individuals

Notes

_____

_____

_____

_____

组织发展测试

幸福感

案例研究：工作生活质量问卷

伦敦一家公司的人力资源经理增加了对员工福利的关注。员工的年度出勤率考勤表明员工的下班时间远远早于应该的离岗时间，分析之后，原因是过大的压力、焦虑和其他疾病，还有员工对企业工作生活质量的抱怨。

经过召开紧急会议，公司决定进行组织审计，评估健康和幸福感氛围。选用的是**工作生活质量问卷**，这可以在以下层面使用：

- 整个组织
- 较小团体的员工
- 与个人共同工作时

TESTING FOR ORGANISATIONAL DEVELOPMENT

WELL-BEING

QUALITY OF WORKING LIFE QUESTIONNAIRE

Unlike the other tests mentioned throughout this pocketbook, no formal training is required to use this questionnaire.

The questionnaire measures seven aspects of working life:

1. Support from a manager or supervisor.
2. Freedom from work-related stress.
3. Salary and additional benefits.
4. Job satisfaction, challenge, use of skill and autonomy.
5. Relationships with work colleagues.
6. Involvement and responsibility at work.
7. Communication, decision making and job security.

Used with the kind permission of ASE.

Notes

_____

_____

_____

_____

_____

组织发展测试

幸福感

工作生活质量问卷

不同于本书提到的其他测试，使用这个问卷不需要正式培训。

问卷从七个方面测试工作生活：

1. 经理或主管的支持
2. 没有与工作相关的压力
3. 薪水和附加福利
4. 工作满足感、挑战、技能的使用和自主权
5. 与同事的人际关系
6. 对工作的参与感和责任感
7. 沟通、决策和工作保障

经 ASE 许可使用。

TESTING FOR ORGANISATIONAL DEVELOPMENT

WELL-BEING

CASE STUDY: QUALITY OF WORKING LIFE QUESTIONNAIRE

Individuals rated their responses on a five point scale: from strongly agree to strongly disagree. The results were then processed by a software program and reports generated that gave the HR manager a good overview of the perceived quality of working life.

The results showed that there was indeed a higher than normal level of dissatisfaction across the seven aspects measured. The company decided to introduce a well-being programme including in-house relaxation therapists, a gym facility and employee assistance programmes. It was also decided that after six months the quality of life questionnaire would be run again to compare any changes in the perceived quality of working life across the organisation.

"Just off to the well-being centre for a massage, boss....."

Used with the kind permission of ASE.

Notes

组织发展测试

幸福感

案例研究：工作生活质量问卷

每个人的回答包括五个量度：从强烈赞同到完全不赞同。结果经过软件程序处理，生成对工作生活质量的全面评估报告，提交给人力资源经理。

结果显示，测试的七个方面，不满意度均高于正常值。公司决定引进福利计划，包括内部放松治疗师、健身房设备和员工帮助项目。同时决定 6 个月后再次进行工作生活问卷调查，比较对组织工作生活质量感受的变化。

经 ASE 许可使用。

"老板，我刚去了幸福感中心做了个按摩……"

TESTING FOR ORGANISATIONAL DEVELOPMENT

MANAGEMENT DEVELOPMENT

A series of questionnaires designed to measure management style, motivation, talent and preferred culture, known as **Saville Consulting Wave®** was launched by Saville Consulting in 2005. The Professional Styles Expert Report, developed by Professor Peter Saville (MacIver et. al., 2006) measures participants in three ways:

1. Exploration of **motives, preferences, needs and talents** in critical work clusters, eg:
   - **Thought** – vision, judgement and evaluation
   - **Influence** – leadership, impact and communication
   - **Adaptability** – support, resilience and flexibility
   - **Delivery** – structure, drive and implementation

2. A measure of Predicted Culture/Environment Fit, indicating those aspects of the culture of the organisation, job and environment likely to enhance or inhibit a person's success.

3. The Competency Potential Report, linking the questionnaire responses to real data on work performance validated on over 1,000 professionals giving a unique prediction of candidates' likely strengths and limitations in 36 key performance/competency areas.

Used with the kind permission of Saville Consulting Group Ltd. (See page 241 for full reference)

Notes

管理发展

萨维尔咨询测评®是专门测试管理方式、动机、才能和文化偏好的系列问卷，由萨维尔咨询公司于 2005 年发行。彼得·萨维尔教授（麦基弗尔，2006）研发的职业风格专家报告从三个方面测试参与者：

1. 探索关键工作集群的**动机、偏好、需求和才能**，例如：

- **想法**——愿景、判断和评价
- **影响**——领导力、影响和沟通
- **适应性**——支持、弹性和灵活性
- **传达**——结构、驱动力和执行

2. 测试预计文化／环境契合，表明有可能提高或抑制个人成功的组织文化、工作和环境

3. 胜任潜力报告，把问卷回答与真实数据相结合，针对 1000 名专业人员的有效工作绩效，给出 36 个关键绩效／能力领域应聘者优劣势的独特预测。

经萨维尔咨询集团允许使用（全部参考信息见 241 页）。

TESTING FOR ORGANISATIONAL DEVELOPMENT

MANAGEMENT DEVELOPMENT
CASE STUDY: SAVILLE CONSULTING WAVE

Simon was being considered for a management role in his engineering company. The People Development director asked him to complete **Wave Professional Styles**. They then reviewed his Competency Potential Profile together. Under the Influence cluster, Simon scored highly on Providing Leadership (Making Decisions, Directing People, Empowering Individuals) indicating suitability for management. Scores for Building Relationships (Interacting with People, Establishing Rapport, Impressing People) were, however, all low.

Simon acknowledged that these areas would need greater focus in a future management position. It was agreed to look at how to develop his skills through a combination of coaching and external training. His readiness for promotion would then be reviewed six months later, when he was more likely to be ready for the new people responsibilities.

Other applications for Wave in the workplace are in **selection**: compatibility and fit, planning, induction, improving motivation, job satisfaction and retention; **development**: aligning motives and talents, building successful teams and improving commitment, and **change**: aligning people to culture change, identifying barriers to change and closing the gap between preferred and actual culture.

Used with the kind permission of Saville Consulting Group Ltd.

Notes

_____

_____

_____

_____

_____

组织发展测试

管理发展

案例研究：萨维尔咨询测评

　　西蒙是其所在的工程公司的管理职位人选，人才发展主管要他完成**萨维尔职场风格测评**，再一起评估他的胜任潜力报告。在影响力方面，西蒙在提供领导力（做决策，指挥人员，授权给个人）上的得分很高，表明适合管理岗位。但是，在建立关系（与人互动，建立良好关系，给人留下印象）方面的得分都很低。

　　西蒙承认在未来的管理岗位上要对这些地方多加注意。公司决定观察他如何结合教练和外部培训培养这些技能。6个月后，等他准备好承担新的人际责任后，再考核他是否适合晋升。

　　萨维尔在职场中的其他应用主要在**选择方面**：相容和适合，计划，就职，提高积极性，工作满意度和员工保持率；**发展方面**：匹配动机和才能，建立成功团队，增加投入；**改变方面**：使员工契合文化的变化，识别变革的障碍，弥合偏好文化同实际文化的差距。

经萨维尔咨询集团允许使用。

TESTING FOR TEAMS

团队测试

TESTING FOR TEAMS

WHY USE TEAM TESTS?

INNOVATION & TEAMWORKING

Teams are increasingly seen as one of the best ways to achieve innovation and improvement in business life. But just calling a diverse group of people a team doesn't always lead to good teamwork. Furthermore, with the challenges of globalisation and rapid change, the single element in the workplace that is likely to remain constant is the need for people to be able to function in work-based groups or teams.

Team tests can be very useful in the following areas:

- Developing stronger, more unified teams who all share the same vision
- Identifying team strengths and weaknesses
- Identifying each team member's role within the team
- Providing role clarity about what is expected from each team member
- Empowering the team's self-awareness through knowing their own individual strengths and limitations, and becoming comfortable with each other
- Strengthening the teams that move the organisation forward, particularly Senior Management Teams
- Identifying teams that integrate well within the wider organisation
- Valuing the diversity of group members and what they have to offer

Notes

_____

_____

_____

_____

_____

团队测试

为什么使用团队测试？

创新与团队精神

在商务生活中，团队被逐渐视为实现创新和发展的最佳方式之一，但是仅仅把一个由各种人组成的队伍称为团队并不一定能带来良好的团队合作。而且，随着全球化和迅速变革带来的挑战，人们需要在基于工作的群体或团队中发挥作用，这可能是职场中唯一保持不变的要素。

团队测试在以下方面非常有用：

- 使拥有共同理想的队伍更加强大、团结
- 识别团队的优势和弱势
- 识别每位团队成员在团队中的作用
- 提供对每位成员明确的角色期望
- 通过认识每位成员自身的优势和局限，让团队了解自己，从而更为融洽地相处
- 巩固能促进组织发展的团队，尤其是高级管理团队
- 识别能够较好融入组织的团队
- 注重团队成员的多样性和他们能发挥的作用

TESTING FOR TEAMS

WHY USE TEAM TESTS?

A team role is defined by Dr Meredith Belbin as: *'a tendency to behave, contribute and interrelate with others in a particular way'*.

In a well run hotel the owner ensures that she employs staff to handle reception, cooking, cleaning and waiting, ie different people to fit different roles to ensure the comfort of the customers. The principles of teamworking rely on having a balanced team of people **fulfilling different functions**, in the same way that they bring their different behaviours to work.

Research has also shown that different combinations of behaviours can create more effective team members. For example, if everyone on the team is bursting with creative ideas but no one likes routine and detail, then the team is likely to be heading for failure. It is, therefore, very important **to have a balanced team taking up different roles** to enhance team performance.

The next case study will demonstrate the significance of having different team roles.

Notes

_____

_____

_____

_____

_____

团队测试

为什么使用团队测试?

　　梅雷迪思·贝尔滨博士对团队角色这样定义:"以某种特定方式做事、发挥作用和与他人互动的倾向。"

　　一家经营有道的酒店,店主要确保雇用的员工,能负责接待、烹饪、清洁和服侍,即不同的人适应不同的角色从而保证为顾客提供舒适的服务。团队合作原则依赖于拥有一个均衡的团队,队员能够**履行不同的职责**,正如他们将不同的行为带到工作中一样。

　　研究表明,不同的行为组合能够创造出更高效的团队成员。例如,如果团队中的每个人都充满创意,但是没有人喜欢做常规琐碎的事情,这个团队就可能遭遇失败。因此,要提高团队绩效,一个**拥有不同角色的均衡团队**是很重要的。

　　下面这个案例研究将证明不同团队角色的重要性。

TESTING FOR TEAMS

TEAM ROLES

CASE STUDY: BELBIN TEAM ROLES INVENTORY

The owner of a hotel feels that she and her staff of eight people would benefit from a better understanding of their identity as a team. The purpose would be to help the individuals understand:

● Where their strengths lie
● What role they contribute to the team as a whole
● The roles that others play

It will help the team to work more smoothly if each team member understands the roles of others and where they all complement each other.

A business psychologist was called in and the whole team was asked to complete the **Belbin Team Roles Inventory**.

Notes

_____

_____

_____

_____

_____

团队测试

团队角色

案例研究：贝尔宾团队角色量表

　　一家酒店的老板认为她和她的八个员工如果对他们这个团队有更好的了解，会从中受益。这个目标会帮助每个人理解：

- 他们的优势在哪里
- 他们在整个团队中扮演的角色
- 其他人扮演的角色

　　每个团队成员都了解其他人的角色和彼此相互补充的地方有助于团队更好地运作。

　　他们聘请的企业心理学家要求他们整个团队完成**贝尔宾团队角色量表**。

TESTING FOR TEAMS

TEAM ROLES

Dr Meredith Belbin and his team of researchers studied the behaviour of managers from all over the world. They wanted to answer the question: why do some teams perform better than others?

The research highlighted the fact that people in teams tend to assume different 'team roles' and the role that each individual plays within the team underlies the team success. Therefore each team member has a vital contribution to make.

The nine team roles, including the latest addition of 'Specialist', are presented on the following pages, which show how each role contributes to the team and what their allowable weaknesses might be.

Notes

_____

_____

_____

_____

_____

团队测试

团队角色

梅雷迪恩·贝尔宾博士和他的研究团队分析了世界各地的经理的行为，他们希望能够找到这个问题的答案：为什么某些团队比其他团队更优秀？

这项研究突出了一个事实，团队成员倾向于承担不同的"团队角色"，每个人在团队中扮演的角色构成了团队获得成功的基础，因此每个成员所发挥的作用都很重要。

下面几页展示了九种团队角色，包括最新增加的"专家"角色，说明了每个角色是如何对团队做出贡献的和他们可能存在的可容许缺陷。

TESTING FOR TEAMS

THE 9 BELBIN TEAM ROLES
SUMMARY DESCRIPTIONS

1. PLANT

Contribution to the team: Creative, imaginative, unorthodox, able to solve difficult problems.

Allowable weakness: Can ignore incidentals, and may be too preoccupied to communicate effectively.

2. RESOURCE INVESTIGATOR

Contribution to the team: Extrovert, enthusiastic, communicative, explores opportunities, develops contacts.

Allowable weakness: Over-optimistic, loses interest once initial enthusiasm has passed.

Notes

_____

_____

_____

_____

_____

团队测试

9种贝尔宾团队角色

总述

1. 创新者

对团队的贡献：富有创造力，想象力，不拘于成规，能够解决困难问题

可容许缺陷：忽视偶然事件，过于固执己见，不能有效沟通

2. 资源调查者

对团队的贡献：性格外向，充满热情，善于交际，探索机会，发展关系网络

可容许缺陷：过分乐观，初始热情殆尽后会失去兴趣

TESTING FOR TEAMS

THE 9 BELBIN TEAM ROLES

SUMMARY DESCRIPTIONS

3. CO-ORDINATOR

Contribution to the team: Mature, confident, a good chairperson, clarifies goals, promotes decision-making, delegates well.

Allowable weakness: Can be seen as manipulative, offloads personal work.

4. SHAPER

Contribution to the team: Challenging, dynamic, thrives on pressure, the drive and courage to overcome obstacles.

Allowable weakness: Prone to provocation, offends people's feelings.

Notes

_____

_____

_____

_____

_____

9 种贝尔宾团队角色

总述

3. 协调者

对团队的贡献：成熟，自信，优秀的领导者，目标清晰，促进决策，善于授权

可容许缺陷：可能被认为善于操控别人，推脱个人工作

4. 塑造者

对团队的贡献：具有挑战性，充满活力，直面压力，有动力和勇气克服障碍

可容许缺陷：易受挑衅，冒犯他人

THE 9 BELBIN TEAM ROLES
SUMMARY DESCRIPTIONS

5. MONITOR EVALUATOR

Contribution to the team: Sober, strategic and discerning, sees all options, judges accurately.

Allowable weakness: Lacks drive and ability to inspire others.

6. TEAMWORKER

Contribution to the team: Co-operative, mild, perceptive and diplomatic, listens, builds, averts friction.

Allowable weakness: Indecisive in crunch situations.

Notes

_____

_____

_____

_____

_____

团队测试

9 种贝尔宾团队角色

总述

5. 监控评估者

对团队的贡献：冷静，有战略眼光，观察力敏锐，能看到所有的备选方案，判断准确

可容许缺陷：缺乏动力和鼓舞他人的能力

6. 团队协作者

对团队的贡献：有合作精神，温和，洞察力敏锐，有交际技能，善于倾听，建立关系，避免摩擦

可容许缺陷：关键时刻犹豫不决

版权归贝尔宾®所有，经同意转载。

TESTING FOR TEAMS

THE 9 BELBIN TEAM ROLES
SUMMARY DESCRIPTIONS

7. IMPLEMENTER

Contribution to the team: Disciplined, reliable, conservative and efficient, turns ideas into practical actions.

Allowable weakness: Somewhat inflexible, slow to respond to new possibilities.

8. COMPLETER FINISHER

Contribution to the team: Painstaking, conscientious, anxious, searches out errors and omissions, delivers on time.

Allowable weakness: Inclined to worry unduly, reluctant to delegate.

Notes

_____

_____

_____

_____

_____

团队测试

9 种贝尔宾团队角色

总述

7. 执行者

对团队的贡献：遵守纪律，值得信赖，保守，效率高，善于把想法付诸实践

可容许缺陷：有时不够灵活，对可能的新情况反应迟钝

8. 完成者

对团队的贡献：刻苦，认真，有紧迫感，发现错误和遗漏，准时完成任务

可容许缺陷：有可能过度焦虑，不愿意授权

THE 9 BELBIN TEAM ROLES
SUMMARY DESCRIPTIONS

9. SPECIALIST

Contribution to the team: Single-minded, self-starting, dedicated, provides knowledge and skills in rare supply.

Allowable weakness: Contributes on only a narrow front, dwells on technicalities.

Notes

_____

_____

_____

_____

_____

团队测试

9 种贝尔宾团队角色

总述

9. 专家

对团队的贡献：一心一意，自我激发，敬业，提供宝贵的知识和技能

可容许缺陷：只在狭隘的专门领域有贡献，专业性过强

TESTING FOR TEAMS

TEAM ROLES

CASE STUDY: BELBIN TEAM ROLES INVENTORY RESULTS

In the hotel, the Belbin results showed the following job functions matching the corresponding roles:

- Owner (1) – Shaper
- Manager (1) – Co-ordinator
- Receptionists (x 2) – Resource Investigator & Teamworker
- Chef (1) – Specialist
- Head Waiter (1) – Completer Finisher
- Waiter (1) – Teamworker
- Kitchen Staff (x 2) – Teamworkers

The team has the right mix of personnel. The owner (Shaper) provides the necessary drive and energy and works well with the manager (Co-ordinator) who can understand the owner's needs and delegate accordingly. The hospitality industry needs plenty of teamworkers, which this team has, to ensure good customer service.

The team lacks an Implementer which might mean poor organisation and use of time. The hotel does achieve results, however. Since individuals rarely have just one preferred behaviour, it could be that the Implementer role features highly on a number of people's profiles. The lack of a Plant in the team is not necessarily a bad thing in this environment, where new ideas and creative solutions to difficult business problems are not really required.

Notes

_____

_____

_____

_____

_____

团队测试

团队角色

案例研究：贝尔宾团队角色量表结果

贝尔宾量表的结果表明酒店中与以下工作职能相匹配的角色：

- 店主（1）：塑造者
- 经理（1）：协调者
- 接待员（×2）：资源调查者
  & 团队协作者
- 厨师（1）：专家
- 领班（1）：完成者
- 服务员（1）：团队协作者
- 厨房员工（×2）：团队协作者

　　这个团队具备恰当的人员搭配组合。店主（塑造者）提供必要的动力和能量，与经理（协调者）配合良好，经理了解店主的需求并作出相应的任务委派。就像这个团队一样，酒店业需要大量的团队协作者来确保优质的客户服务。

　　这个团队缺少执行者，意味着组织架构和时间利用不够好。但是，酒店确实有盈利，因为每个人几乎不可能只有一种偏好行为，有可能执行者的角色体现在很多人身上。缺少创新者在这种环境下并不一定是坏事，因为这里并不十分需要新创意和创新的解决方案应对商业难题。

TESTING FOR TEAMS

TEAM BUILDING

CASE STUDY: MYERS-BRIGGS TYPE INDICATOR®

The next popular team test we will be looking at is often adopted for team building purposes as well as for personal and organisational development.

A large international construction company has extended its operations to Dubai, and wants a team of people based there to oversee building standards. The HR department decided to run a team building workshop for the five members of the new team, who would be relocating to Dubai from the UK, US and Canada. For the workshop, they chose the world renowned team building tool, **Myers-Briggs Type Indicator® (MBTI®)**.

The MBTI® tool is a personality test designed to assist an individual in identifying some significant preferences. Katharine Briggs and her daughter Isabel Briggs developed the indicator during the Second World War and its scales follow from Carl Jung's themes in his work *Psychological Types*.

The questionnaire is un-timed, self report and asks respondents to choose between two opposing courses of action, or two words, depending on what they feel is closest to their natural preference. These preferences are presented next.

Notes

_____

_____

_____

_____

_____

团队测试

团队建设

案例研究：迈尔斯－布里格斯类型指标®

接下来的这个团队测试颇受欢迎，不仅常常被用于个人和组织的发展，也用来进行团队建设。

一家大型国际建筑公司将业务拓展到了迪拜，并希望有一个团队在那里监督建筑标准，新团队的五个人要从英国、美国和加拿大调到迪拜。人力资源部门决定为五名成员开展团队建设工作坊，选择了全球知名的团队建设工具**迈尔斯－布里格斯类型指标®**(**MBTI®**)。

MBTI®是一个人格测试工具，旨在帮助个人识别一些显著偏好。凯瑟琳·布里格斯和女儿伊莎贝尔·布里格斯在二战期间创造了这个指标，其量度遵照卡尔·荣格在其著作《心理类型》中的主题。

问卷是不计时的自我报告，要求回答者按照最接近自己的自然偏好，在相反的两种做法或者两个词语中做选择。这些偏好如下页所示。

迈尔斯-布里格斯类型指标，迈尔斯-布里格斯和MBTI是迈尔斯-布里格斯类型指标机构在美国和其他国家的商标和注册商标。经允许使用。

TESTING FOR TEAMS

WHAT THE MBTI® TOOL MEASURES

Extraversion (E) – Prefers to draw their energy from the outside world of activity, people and things.

Or

Introversion (I) – Prefers to draw their energy from the inner world of reflections, thoughts, feelings and ideas.

Sensing (S) – Prefers to focus on the present and on concrete information gained from their five senses for perceiving the world around them.

Or

Intuition (N) – Prefers to focus on the future and uses their intuitive side or 'sixth sense' to focus on relationships and possibilities.

Notes

_____

_____

_____

_____

_____

团队测试

MBTI® 工具测什么

外向（E）——倾向于从活动、人员和事情等外在世界获得能量

或者

内向（I）——倾向于从反思、思考、感受和想法的内部世界获得能量

感觉（S）——倾向于关注当前的、具体的信息，通过五官感受周围世界

或者

直觉（N）——倾向于关注未来，通过直觉或"第六感"关注关系和可能性

迈尔斯-布里格斯类型指标，迈尔斯-布里格斯和MBTI是迈尔斯-布里格斯类型指标机构在美国和其他国家的商标和注册商标。经允许使用。

TESTING FOR TEAMS

WHAT THE MBTI® TOOL MEASURES

Thinking (T) – Prefers to base their decisions on logic and objective analysis of cause and effect.

Or

Feeling (F) – Prefers to base decisions on a valuing process, considering what is important to people.

Judging (J) – Prefers a planned, organised approach to life with quick closure.

Or

Perceiving (P) – Prefers a flexible, spontaneous approach and to keep their options open.

Notes

团队测试

MBTI® 工具测什么

思考（T）——倾向于
以逻辑和对因果的
客观分析为基础做决定

或者

情感（F）——倾向于
以评估过程为基础做决定，
考虑对人重要的方面

判断（J）——倾向于
有计划、有组织的
生活方式，快速决策

或者

知觉（P）——倾向于
灵活的、自发的方式，
保持选择的开放性

迈尔斯-布里格斯类型指标，迈尔斯-布里格斯和 MBTI 是迈尔斯-布里格斯类型指标机构在美国和其他国家的商标和注册商标。经允许使用。

TESTING FOR TEAMS

TEAM BUILDING

CASE STUDY MYERS-BRIGGS TYPE INDICATOR® RESULTS

Prior to the workshop, the five participants undertook the tests electronically (using confidential login and passwords). The results (see next page) indicated a substantial amount of similarity among the five members of the new team.

The performance of **highly similar** teams can vary, with some performing quite well and others struggling. Whether a team with a high similarity is successful or not depends on two things:

1. How well the team type fits with the approach required by their task or project.
2. How aware the team is of its blind spots, ie the preferences not covered by anyone on the team.

The results show a team type of ESTJ, although only two of the five have this full profile. (The team type is derived by counting the number of team members with each preference.) What is important here is that the sum of the individual MBTI® profiles forms an overall team style and the task will be completed within that team style of ESTJ, which will be different from some of the team members' preferences.

Myers-Briggs Type Indicator, Myers-Briggs and MBTI are trademarks or registered trademarks of the Myers-Briggs Type Indicator Trust in the United States and other countries. Used with permission.

 Notes

_____

_____

_____

_____

_____

团队建设

迈尔斯－布里格斯类型指标®案例研究结果

工作坊开始之前，五名参与者进行了在线测试（用户名和密码保密）。结果（见下页）表明新团队的五名成员有极大的相似性。

高相似度团队的表现各不相同，有些表现得很出色，而有些则表现得差强人意。一个高度相似的团队成功与否取决于以下两个方面：

1. 团队类型和其任务、项目对团队的要求相匹配程度怎样
2. 团队对自己的盲区，即团队成员都不具有的倾向的认识程度如何

结果显示他们是 ESTJ 团队类型，尽管五个人中只有两个完全符合这种类型。（团队类型是通过计算每一项偏好的团队成员数得出的）。重要的是，整个团队的风格由个人 MBTI 特征的总和所构成，并且任务由 ESTJ 类型的团队完成，这与一些队员的偏好是不同的。

迈尔斯-布里格斯类型指标，迈尔斯-布里格斯和 MBTI 是迈尔斯-布里格斯类型指标机构在美国和其他国家的商标和注册商标。经允许使用。

TESTING FOR TEAMS

TEAM BUILDING

CASE STUDY MYERS-BRIGGS TYPE INDICATOR® RESULTS

ISTJ ①	ISFT	INFJ	**INTJ** ①
ISTP	ISFP	INFP	INTP
ESTP	ESFP	ENFP	ENTP
ESTJ ②	**ESFJ** ①	ENFJ	ENTJ

Extraversion	3
Introversion	2
Sensing	4
Intuition	1
Thinking	4
Feeling	1
Judging	5
Perceiving	0

> Resulting in a
> pooled set of
> preferences of
> **ESTJ**

The team has no cover of the **Perceiving** preference, suggesting they may have a lack of flexibility and spontaneity; there may only be limited cover of **Intuition** (future focus and possibilities) and **Feeling** (basing decisions on values and subjective evaluation).

These points will be raised by the facilitator in the team briefing session in order to look at ways forward for the team to help in the overall success of the business.

Myers-Briggs Type Indicator, Myers-Briggs and MBTI are trademarks or registered trademarks of the Myers-Briggs Type Indicator Trust in the United States and other countries. Used with permission.

Notes

团队测试

团队建设

迈尔斯－布里格斯类型指标®案例研究结果

ISTJ①	ISFT	INFJ	**INTJ**①	外向	3	
				内向	2	
ISTP	ISFP	INFP	INTP	感觉	4	结果是 ESTJ 型
				直觉	1	
ESTP	ESFP	ENFP	ENTP	思考	4	
				情感	1	
ESTJ②	**ESFJ**①	ENFJ	ENTJ	判断	5	
				知觉	0	

这个团队缺少**知觉**偏向，意味着可能缺乏灵活性和自发性；并且仅有有限的**直觉**（对未来和可能性的关注）和**情感**（基于价值观和客观评估做出决策）倾向。

在团队简报会上，协调人会提出这些问题，帮助团队找出方法，促进企业走向成功。

迈尔斯-布里格斯类型指标，迈尔斯-布里格斯和 MBTI 是迈尔斯-布里格斯类型指标机构在美国和其他国家的商标和注册商标。经允许使用。

TESTING FOR TEAMS

HIGH SIMILARITY TEAMS

High similarity amongst team members is normally associated with:

- Finishing tasks more quickly
- Failing to make good use of the resources of the team; perhaps not identifying or using the talents of the right person for the task
- Producing more traditional, less original, solutions to problems
- Producing more limited or constrained solutions than do highly dissimilar teams, as judged by external criteria
- Pressure within the team to solve problems by consensus, which may inhibit the expression of unique individual solution

On the following pages are lists of possible strengths and limitations for an ESTJ team and a contrasting INFP team.

Notes

团队测试

高相似度团队

团队成员之间的高相似度通常会意味着：

- 更快速地完成任务
- 不能充分利用团队资源；或许不能识别、利用适合的人完成任务
- 制定的问题解决方案更为传统、不够新颖
- 相比高度不相似的团队，若以外部标准衡量，制定的解决方案更局限、更受约束
- 通过统一意见来解决问题所带来的内部压力，或许会抑制个人表达独特的解决方案

下面几页列出了 ESTJ 型团队和对比的 INFP 型团队的优势和局限。

CONTRASTING TEAMS

ESTJ

Possible strengths:

- Decisive and outspoken
- Bases decisions on known facts
- Structured and organised
- Has clear performance expectations
- Achieves practical results
- Keeps bottom line in sight

Possible limitations:

- May reject new ideas
- May be unaware of new trends
- May override important long-range factors for short-term goals (often financial)
- May make decisions without all the information
- May not consider how decisions will affect key stakeholders

Notes

_____

_____

_____

_____

_____

団队测试

对比团队

ESTJ

潜在优势：

- 果断，直言不讳
- 将决策建立在已知事实上
- 结构化，组织化
- 具有清晰的业绩预期
- 取得实际的结果
- 锁定盈亏底线

潜在局限：

- 可能排斥新的想法
- 可能意识不到新的趋势
- 可能因（通常是财务上的）短期目标而无视重要的长期因素
- 可能在信息不足时做决策
- 可能考虑不到决策对重要利益相关者的影响

CONTRASTING TEAMS

INFP

Possible strengths:
- Creative
- Adaptable
- Counselling approach
- Gently persuasive
- Sense of purpose

Possible limitations:
- May get overwhelmed by possibilities
- May overlook important facts
- May not consider logical consequences of each alternative
- May be overly influenced by what others in the team want
- May be put off making decisions

Notes

_____

_____

_____

_____

_____

団队测试

对比团队

INFP

潜在优势：　　　　**潜在局限：**

- 富有创造力
- 适应性强
- 咨询的方式
- 温和的说服力
- 目标感

- 可能被各种可能性压垮
- 可能忽略重要的事实
- 可能考虑不到每个选择后面的逻辑后果
- 可能过多受到团队其他成员期望的影响
- 可能延迟进行决策

TESTING FOR TEAMS

CONCLUSION

The Belbin instrument and the MBTI® instrument look at teams in different ways. Belbin looks at individual job roles first and the type of tasks that are naturally preferred; the MBTI® tool looks more at personality as a whole and the way that team members' personality preferences group together to make up a team, following the preferred style of the aggregate of those preferences.

As mentioned earlier, a team operates most effectively when a balanced spread of preferences is demonstrated. Do not assume that everyone should have the same type preference.

A team review session should point out possible strengths and limitations while making it clear that type differences are very important. It is particularly important that areas affecting work tasks that are not, or are insufficiently, covered, eg Plant and Implementer in our Belbin example, and INFP preferences in our MBTI® example, should be discussed with team members and management.

Finally, possible blind spots and conflict areas should be confronted and dealt with through discussion with other individuals with different type preferences.

Notes

_____

_____

_____

_____

_____

团队测试

结论

　　贝尔宾工具和 MBTI®工具用不同的方式观察团队，贝尔宾首先观察的是个人工作角色和自然偏向的任务类型；MBTI 工具更多观察的是整体个性和包括成员的团队整体的人格偏好，即由这些偏好组合成的偏好方式。

　　正如之前提到的，一个团队具备均衡的偏好时，绩效最佳。不要假定每个人都该有同样的偏好。

　　团队评审会应指出潜在的优势和局限，同时表明偏好类型差异的重要性。尤其重要的是，应与队员和管理层就没有或未被完全涵盖但又会影响到工作任务的领域进行商讨，如在贝尔宾案例中的创新者和执行者，以及 MBTI®案例中的 INFP 倾向。

　　最后，应该通过与其他具有不同类型偏好的个人讨论，正视潜在的盲点和有冲突的地方，并处理这些问题。

TESTING FOR PERSONAL DEVELOPMENT

个人发展测试

TESTING FOR PERSONAL DEVELOPMENT

AT THE CROSSROADS

It is perfectly normal for all of us to want to take a pause in life, reflect on where we are going, to re-appraise our lives, and make decisions about the future before moving on. Occasionally life events may force us to do this, but it is quite natural to want to change just for a change!

At these times we need to address three main questions:

- Where are we now?
- Where do we want to go?
- How do we get there?

Where are we now?

Where do we want to go?

How do we get there?

Notes

_____

_____

_____

_____

_____

个人发展测试

十字路口

生活中我们想暂停一下，想想自己要去哪里，重新审视自己的生活，做出关于未来的决定，然后再继续前进，这是完全正常的。

有时候生活会迫使我们这样做，但因为想要改变而改变也是相当正常的！

这种情况下，我们需要解决三个主要问题：

· 我们现在在哪里？

· 我们想要去哪里？

· 我们怎样到那里？

TESTING FOR PERSONAL DEVELOPMENT

WHY PSYCHOMETRIC TESTING?

At these important, life-changing, 'crossroad' times psychometric testing can provide useful signposts. Psychologists tell us that most behaviour is not accidental; it is caused and put into action by our motivation and feelings of satisfying needs, eg:

- Drink when thirsty
- Eat when hungry
- Sleep when tired
- Laugh when happy

A very useful starting point is to use psychometric testing to examine two aspects of our temperament: motivation and personality. Fortunately psychometric test publishers have provided some excellent, valid and reliable instruments to measure these two attributes. We will start by looking at **motivation and a motivational inventory.**

Notes

个人发展测试

为什么要做心理测试？

　　在这些重要的、改变生活的"十字路口"，心理测试能提供有用的指示。心理学家告诉我们，大部分行为都不是偶然发生的，而是由人的动机和满足需要的感觉引起从而付诸行动的，例如：

- 渴了时喝水
- 饿了时吃饭
- 累了时睡觉
- 乐了时大笑

　　利用心理测试检验自己性格的两方面：动机与人格，这是非常有益的起点。幸运的是心理测试出版者提供了一些良好、有效、可信赖的工具来测试这两个特质。我们先来看**动机和动机量表**。

TESTING FOR PERSONAL DEVELOPMENT

MOTIVATION TESTS

Motivation is included here under individual development because in many respects motivation guides our activities throughout the working week, from waking up in the morning to going to bed at night.

When a person is more motivated they:

- Work more productively
- Contribute more to the organisation
- Are more likely to achieve their full potential
- Will gain greater satisfaction from their job
- Have an enhanced feeling of well-being

Unlocking the key to motivation can be a difficult process because all individuals are motivated by different things.

Notes

个人发展测试

动机测试

在这里，动机归在了个人发展里，因为动机会在许多方面引导我们整个工作周的活动，从早上起床到晚上睡觉。

当一个人有更加积极的动力时，他们：

- 工作更有成效
- 对组织贡献更多
- 更有可能实现全部潜力
- 从工作中获得更大的满足
- 幸福感增加

因为每个人会被不同的事物所影响，所以解开动机的秘密不那么容易。

TESTING FOR PERSONAL DEVELOPMENT

MOTIVATION TESTS

Abraham Maslow's Hierarchy of Needs theory was one of the first motivation theories to be applied to individuals at work. Maslow said that people's wants and needs guide behaviour. According to Maslow, a need influences a person's activities at that level until it has been satisfied, and then the superordinate level need is sought. His theory places five needs in an ascending hierarchy, making the assumption that basic needs are met first. This applies to having food and water, a roof over your head, friends, confidence and a need to self-actualise, a posh word for achieving your life dreams! It is at this self-actualisation point that you are supposed to have reached your full potential as an individual.

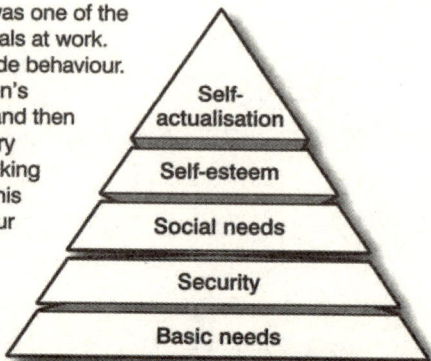

Self-actualisation

Self-esteem

Social needs

Security

Basic needs

It is important to understand what motivates people at work in order to understand how to unlock their full potential, increase productivity and enable them to reach that summit.

Notes

_____

_____

_____

_____

_____

个人发展测试

动机测试

　　亚伯拉罕·马斯洛的需求层次理论是最早应用于职场个人的激励理论之一。马斯洛认为，人的欲望和需求引导行为。根据马斯洛的理论，人的需求会影响所在层次的活动，直到需求得到满足，再寻求更高一级的需求。他假定基本的需求最先得到满足，把五种需求由下到上排列，分别是食物和水、住处、朋友、自信心和对自我实现的需求，也是实现人生梦想的时髦说法！到了实现自我的那一层，作为个体，你才算发挥了全部潜力！

　　弄清楚是什么激励了职场上的个人，这对于了解如何发挥他们的全部潜力、提高生产效率、并使他们到达巅峰状态很重要。

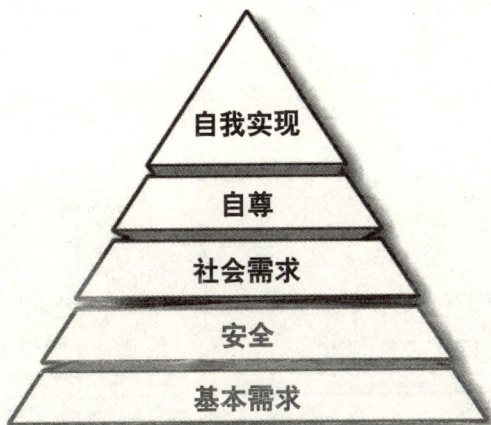

TESTING FOR PERSONAL DEVELOPMENT

MOTIVATION QUESTIONNAIRE

CASE STUDY: SHL MOTIVATION QUESTIONNAIRE (MQ)

Kerri has just joined a large high street bank arranging mortgages. She was snapped up by the bank because she is very numerate and alert with a bubbly personality. A few weeks into her job, however, the manager has started to receive reports that Kerri is upsetting other members of staff. She complains constantly about the boredom of her job which involves arranging mortgages day after day, week after week, in an ongoing and somewhat mundane routine. Her boss asks the HR department for advice. HR recommends profiling Kerri, looking in particular at her sources of motivation which currently appear to be non-existent.

Kerri agrees to complete a motivation questionnaire to see how best her boredom can be dealt with. The **SHL Motivation Questionnaire (MQ)** is chosen because it may hold the key to what would be the best next steps.

This questionnaire measures 18 dimensions of an individual's motivation, and provides a comprehensive understanding of those situations which increase and reduce their motivation. It also helps to determine how long and under what circumstances effort will be maintained.

Notes

_____

_____

_____

_____

_____

个人发展测试

动机调查问卷

案例研究：SHL 动机量表（MQ）

克莉刚刚入职一家商业街的大型银行，处理按揭贷款。银行聘请她是看中她计算能力好，个性活泼。但入职几周后，经理就收到报告说克莉给其他员工造成了困扰。她时常抱怨工作枯燥，日复一日周复一周都在安排按揭，日常工作没完没了又单调。她的老板向人力资源部门寻求建议，人力资源部门建议对克莉进行全面的特征描述，尤其是观察她目前看似不存在的动机来源。

克莉想知道该如何处理自己对工作的厌倦，同意完成动机量表。选择 **SHL 动机量表（MQ）** 是因为它或许能决定下一步该采取的最佳方案是什么。

量表测量的是个人动机的 18 个维度，对那些能增强、削弱动机的情境提供了综合的认识，同时它有助于判断努力会持续多久及在什么情况下保持。

TESTING FOR PERSONAL DEVELOPMENT

MOTIVATION QUESTIONNAIRE
SHL MOTIVATION QUESTIONNAIRE (MQ) 18 DIMENSIONS

Some people may be motivated by **energy and dynamism** – the energy with which an individual approaches tasks:

1. Level of activity – how energy is invested
2. Achievement – need to achieve targets, competition
3. Competition – attempt to out do others
4. Fear of failure – prospect of failure, spears activity
5. Power – need to exercise authority
6. Immersion – need to feel involved
7. Commercial outlook – wants to create wealth and profits

Some people may be motivated by **synergy** – feeling comfortable and at ease with the work environment:

1. Affiliation – thrives on meeting people and team work
2. Recognition – likes good work to be noticed
3. Personal principles – wishing to operate in an ethical manner
4. Ease and security – need to feel secure about their job
5. Personal growth – work should provide opportunities for development

Notes

_____

_____

_____

_____

_____

个人发展测试

动机调查问卷

SHL 动机量表（MQ）的 18 个维度

一些人或许会受到**精力和活力的激励**——即个人用来完成任务的能量：

1. 积极性——如何投入精力
2. 成就——实现目标，竞争的需要
3. 竞争——试图超过他人
4. 害怕失败——失败的可能性激发积极性
5. 权力——行使权力的需要
6. 事业心——需要有参与感
7. 商业意识——希望创造财富和利润

一些人可能受到**协同效应**的激励——在工作环境中感觉舒服自在：

1. 联系——喜欢接触人和团队工作
2. 认可——喜欢出色的工作被他人注意到
3. 个人原则——希望以符合道德的方式做事
4. 轻松和保障——对工作感到安全性的需要
5. 个人成长——工作应该提供发展机会

经 SHL 集团有限公司允许使用。

TESTING FOR PERSONAL DEVELOPMENT

MOTIVATION QUESTIONNAIRE

SHL MOTIVATION QUESTIONNAIRE (MQ) 18 DIMENSIONS

Some people may be motivated by **intrinsic rewards** – values, freedom and autonomy:

1. Interest – values, stimulating or creative work
2. Flexibility – favours a fluid environment without structure
3. Autonomy – need to work independently, organise self

Some people may be motivated by **extrinsic rewards** – loads of money:

1. Material reward – links salary and income to success
2. Progression – needs an upwards career path
3. Status – concerned with position, status and the respect they bring

Notes

个人发展测试

动机调查问卷

SHL 动机量表（MQ）的 18 个维度

一些人可能受到**内部报酬**的激励——价值观、自由和自主：

1. 兴趣——价值观，富有刺激性或创造性的工作
2. 灵活——喜欢无组织的不固定环境
3. 自主——需要独立工作，自我安排

一些人可能受到**外部报酬**的激励——大量金钱：

1. 物质奖励——将薪水、收入和成功挂钩
2. 事业发展——需要上升的职业发展路径
3. 地位——关注职位、身份以及由它们带来的尊重

经 SHL 集团有限公司允许使用。

TESTING FOR PERSONAL DEVELOPMENT

MOTIVATION QUESTIONNAIRE

CASE STUDY: SHL MOTIVATION QUESTIONNAIRE (MQ) RESULTS

During the feedback session, it is evident that Kerri has high scores in the following areas:

- **Achievement and competition** – the need to reach targets as well as work in a competitive environment
- **Fear of failure**
- **Power, immersion and commercial outlook**

It is clear that Kerri has a high level of energy and dynamism, possibly too much for the mundane nature of the role. In discussion with the HR manager, they agree that Kerri is not suited to her current role and, with the agreement of her boss, they decide to transfer her into retail sales. In such a post she can use her energy more appropriately dealing directly with customers, meeting targets and satisfying her need for achievement, immersion and commercial activity. Above all, she will be able to see quite clearly that she is not failing.

Without use of the questionnaire to identify more satisfying areas of work, it is likely that Kerri would have left in search of 'less boring' work or taken up negative attitudes and become disruptive. Either way, the bank would have lost a potentially highly talented performer.

Used with kind permission of SHL Group Ltd.

Notes

_____

_____

_____

_____

_____

个人发展测试

动机调查问卷

案例研究：SHL 动机量表（MQ）结果

在反馈环节，可以清楚地看到克莉在以下方面得分很高：

- **成就和竞争**——对在竞争性环境中工作和实现目标的需求
- **害怕失败**
- **权力、事业心和商业意识**

很明显，克莉具有很高的积极性和活力，这或许对于单调的岗位角色来说过高了。经过与人力资源经理的讨论，一致认为克莉不适合现在的职位。经她的老板同意，他们决定把她调到零售部。这个职位能让她直接接触客户，更好地发挥能力，实现目标从而满足她的成就感，事业心和商业意识。最重要的是，她可以清楚地看到自己没有失败。

如果不用量表来识别出更令人满意的工作范畴，克莉很可能已经离开银行去寻找"不那么枯燥"的工作，或者摆出消极的态度，给公司带来损害。不论怎样，银行都会失去一位有潜力、有才能的人员。

经 SHL 集团有限公司允许使用。

TESTING FOR PERSONAL DEVELOPMENT

PERSONALITY TESTS

We move on to look at personality tests to find the best ways of helping others develop. We have already discussed, in the *Testing for Selection* chapter, the background to personality tests and how difficult it can be to select a test from the hundreds flooding the market place. This may put people off. It is, however, well worth making the effort to assist individuals to reach an understanding of their unique personality.

We have chosen to illustrate a foundation test, one with an acclaimed pedigree of research reliability and validity and of particular use in a personal development and change context.

![Notes]

_____

_____

_____

_____

_____

个人发展测试

人格测试

  下面我们来看一看能帮助找出他人成长最佳方式的人格测试。在"遴选测试"那一章，我们曾讲过人格测试的背景和从市场上成百上千的测试中挑出一种有多么困难。这可能会让人感到泄气。但是，帮助个人理解自己独特的性格值得你付出这样的努力。

  我们选择了一个基础测试来加以说明，这个测试广受好评，具有信度和效度，尤其适用于个人发展和改变的情境。

TESTING FOR PERSONAL DEVELOPMENT

PERSONALITY TESTS

CASE STUDY: ECCOS TEST

Sunita works successfully in a lively sales operation, but has recently married, is starting a family and wishes to explore careers where she can develop her people skills in an environment with young children, so that she can integrate family life more closely with her work and her personality. She is thinking about becoming a nursery teacher. Sunita wishes to understand how she can make this career change through a personal development process. She visits a trained counsellor who suggests using a personality questionnaire as a start.

The personality test chosen has been developed from the **Eysenck Personality Questionnaire**. Hans Eysenck first began developing this test as long ago as 1952 while working at the Maudsley Hospital in London. Dr Barry Cripps and Dr Mark Cook, together with Dr Sybil Eysenck, have produced **ECCOS, The Eysenck, Cripps, Cook, Occupational Scales**, measuring seven aspects of personality. **ECCOS** has three features which distinguish it from most other personality questionnaires: links to psychology in general, very extensive cross-cultural research making it truly pan-cultural and a direct application into the world of work.

Used with kind permission of Eysenck, Cripps, Cook Occupational Scales (2007) www.eccos.co.uk

Notes

个人发展测试

人格测试

案例研究：ECCOS 测试

　　萨尼塔在一家销售公司做得很成功，但最近她结婚组建了家庭。她希望探索新的职业路径，让她能在有幼儿的环境中培养人际技巧，从而把家庭生活更好地同自己的工作和性格相融合。她正在考虑做一名育婴师。萨尼塔想知道如何通过个人发展过程做出职业转变。她拜访了一名受过训练的咨询师，咨询师建议她先做一个性格测试。

　　选用的人格测试是从**艾森克人格问卷**发展而来的。汉斯·艾森克早在 1952 年就开发了这个测试方法，当时他在伦敦毛德斯莱医院工作。巴里·克里普斯博士、马克·库克博士和西比尔·艾森克博士一起创造了 **ECCOS，即艾森克，克里普斯，库克职业量表**，测试性格的七个方面。**ECCOS** 不同于其他性格量表的三个特征是：大体与心理学相关，广泛的跨文化研究使其能适应多种文化，可直接应用到工作中。

经艾森克，克里普斯，库克职业量表（2007）允许使用 www.eccos.co.uk。

TESTING FOR PERSONAL DEVELOPMENT

PERSONALITY TESTS
SEVEN SCALES OF ECCOS

The seven scales are as follows:

1. **Tender-minded:** sociable and caring for people –
   Tough-minded: sometimes alone and not overly concerned with people.
2. **Introvert:** quiet, reliable, doesn't make a fuss –
   Extravert: very sociable, outgoing, seeks stimulation and change.
3. **Stable:** relaxed, calm and controlled –
   Anxious: worries overly about things, may lose control.
4. **Low Impulsive:** looks ahead at consequences –
   Impulsive: may not consider consequences.
5. **Low Venturesome:** cautious, unlikely to take risks –
   Venturesome: true risk-taking behaviour.
6. **Low Empathy:** may not see other person point of view or perspective –
   Empathy: able to understand another person perspective and put self in their shoes.
7. **Social Desirability:** (a faking detector) this is a built in scale which detects whether the test taker has been open and honest with their responses to the test questions, or is seeking perfection.

Used with kind permission of Eysenck, Cripps, Cook Occupational Scales (2007) www.eccos.co.uk

Notes

_____

_____

_____

_____

_____

个人发展测试

人格测试

ECCOS 的七个量度

以下是 ECCOS 的七个量度:

1. **温柔**: 善于交际, 关怀别人

   坚强: 有时候爱独处, 不会过分关注他人

2. **内向型**: 安静, 可信赖, 不引人注目

   外向型: 非常善于交际, 开朗, 寻求刺激和变化

3. **稳重型**: 放松, 冷静, 克制

   焦虑型: 过分担忧事情, 或许会失去控制

4. **不易冲动**: 预见到后果

   冲动: 或许不考虑后果

5. **不爱冒险**: 谨慎, 不喜欢冒险

   冒险型: 冒险行为

6. **低移情**: 不会从他人的角度看问题

   移情: 能够理解其他人的角度, 站在他人角度看问题

7. **社会期许**: (验证是否作假) 这是一个内部量度, 检验受测

   试者的回答是否诚实、没有隐瞒, 还是在追求完美。

经艾森克, 克里普斯, 库克职业量表 (2007) 允许使用 www.eccos.co.uk。

TESTING FOR PERSONAL DEVELOPMENT

PERSONALITY TESTS

CASE STUDY: ECCOS

Sunita completes the personality test and her results are displayed below:

SUNITA'S SCORES

	1	2	3	4	5	6	7	8	9	10	
Tender-minded						■					Tough-minded
Introvert									■		Extravert
Stable				■							Anxious
Low Impulsive								■			Impulsive
Low Venturesome								■			Venturesome
Low Empathy						■					Empathy
Low Social Desirability				■							Social Desirability

Used with kind permission of Eysenck, Cripps, Cook Occupational Scales (2007) www.eccos.co.uk

Notes

个人发展测试

人格测试

案例研究：ECCOS

萨尼塔完成了人格测试，结果如下：

萨尼塔的分数：

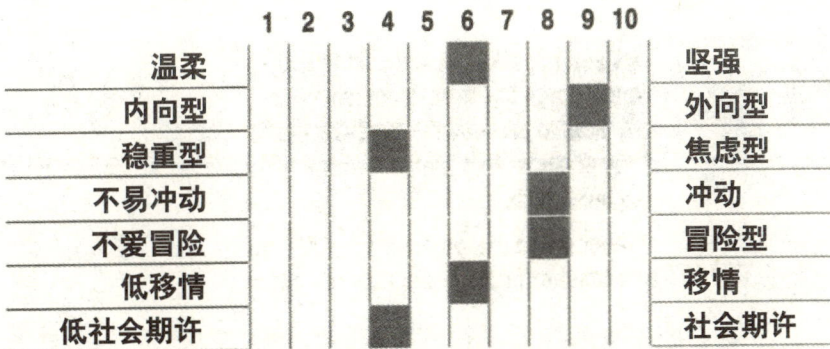

	1	2	3	4	5	6	7	8	9	10	
温柔						■					坚强
内向型									■		外向型
稳重型				■							焦虑型
不易冲动								■			冲动
不爱冒险								■			冒险型
低移情						■					移情
低社会期许				■							社会期许

经艾森克，克里普斯，库克职业量表（2007）允许使用 www.eccos.co.uk。

TESTING FOR PERSONAL DEVELOPMENT

PERSONALITY TESTS

CASE STUDY: ECCOS RESULTS

Sunita reports herself in the middle (6) of the Tough- Tender-minded scale, indicating a level of interest in others, and an ability to take people or leave them. Her score of **9** for Extravert reflects her bubbly, fairly assertive temperament, ready to accept the changes in development she is choosing.

Her score of **4** for Stable will see her taking a fairly calm, even tempered, flexible approach, reasonably able to accept the stresses of teaching. Sunita shows a typical level of empathy (**6**), usually able to see others' points of view and read their feelings. At 4 on the Social Desirability scale, she indicates that she has answered honestly and openly and not tried to fake her results.

Sunita and her counsellor reason that this personality profile can help her positively in her objective of becoming a teacher (though she may need to rein in her impulsiveness for reality checks at times).

The technique of using a personality test in counselling for personal development is a powerful way of 'opening up' the client and uncovering personality trait data of use in helping the client move in new directions.

Used with kind permission of Eysenck, Cripps, Cook Occupational Scales (2007) www.eccos.co.uk

Notes

_____

_____

_____

_____

_____

个人发展测试

人格测试

案例研究：ECCOS 结果

萨尼塔在坚强／温柔这个量度处于中间值（6），表明她对他人有一定程度的关注，与其他人合群也能独处。外向量度为 9 分，反映了她性格活泼、相当自信，乐于接受因为选择带来的发展变化。

稳重量度为 4 分，说明她处事冷静，性情温和，手段灵活，基本能够承受教学压力。萨尼塔是典型的移情（6）类型，通常能理解别人的看法，意识到他人的感受。社会期许量度为 4 分，说明她的回答诚实，没有隐瞒，也没有试图造假。

萨尼塔和她的咨询师认为这个人格剖析图有助于她实现成为教师的目标（尽管她可能需要为了现实状况而偶尔克制自己的冲动）。

在针对个人发展的咨询中，使用人格测试是一种有效的方式，能够"揭秘"客户，发现有助于他们朝着新方向前进的人格特征信息。

经艾森克，克里普斯，库克职业量表（2007）允许使用 www.eccos.co.uk。

TESTING FOR PERSONAL DEVELOPMENT

EI ABILITY TEST

CASE STUDY: MSCEIT

We have already mentioned emotional intelligence in the section on Organisational Development. The following test looks at EI from a completely different perspective.

Andrew is an operations manager for a major organisation. He was informed by his boss that he and his team were going to be relocated from the buzz of the square mile in the heart of the City of London to a less desirable area south of the River Thames.

The move was not without its problems, particularly when it came to uprooting staff from the trendy bars and restaurants they had become attached to. Andrew listened to his team's complaints and understood their feelings very well indeed. However, as each problem was resolved another complaint came up. After a while this had a noticeable effect on the productivity of the group. At this point, Andrew was referred for executive coaching to help him resolve the issues around managing his people.

The coach asked Andrew to complete the **Mayer Salovey Caruso Emotional Intelligence Test (MSCEIT)**, developed by Peter Salovey, John Mayer and David Caruso.

Notes

_____

_____

_____

_____

_____

个人发展测试

EI 能力测试

案例研究：MSCEIT

在组织发展的章节中，我们提到过情商。下面的测试从完全不同的角度来观察情商（EI）。

安德鲁是一家大公司的营运经理，他接到老板的通知，要把他和他的团队从繁华的伦敦金融城调到不那么受人喜欢的泰晤士河以南区域。

这个调动有点问题，尤其是要让员工离开他们已经习惯的时尚酒吧和饭店。安德鲁听到队员的抱怨，也非常理解他们的感受。但是，解决了一个问题，其他的抱怨又出现了。这很快对团队的工作效率造成了明显的影响。这时，有人建议安德鲁请高管教练帮忙解决队员管理的问题。

教练要安德鲁完成由彼特·萨洛维、约翰·梅耶和大卫·克鲁索创造的**梅耶萨洛维克鲁索情商测试（MSCEIT）**。

TESTING FOR PERSONAL DEVELOPMENT

EI ABILITY TEST
THE MSCEIT EMOTIONAL INTELLIGENCE TEST

The MSCEIT test is based on an ability model of emotional intelligence designed to assess the potential (or capacity) for emotionally intelligent behaviour. It takes a very different approach from many of the other psychometric instruments in this pocketbook.

The test authors state that their model defines emotional intelligence as the ability to reason with, and about emotions, and that for optimal performance to take place thinking and feeling have to work together in harmony.

The MSCEIT model consists of the following **Emotional Blueprint**:

1. **Identifying Emotions:** *What emotions are you, and others, experiencing?*
2. **Using Emotions:** *How are these emotions directing attention and influencing thinking?*
3. **Understanding Emotions:** *What caused these emotions and how might they change?*
4. **Managing Emotions:** *What emotional strategies best address the problem?*

Notes

_____

_____

_____

_____

_____

个人发展测试

EI 能力测试

MSCEIT 情商测试

MSCEIT 测试基于一个情商的能力模型，专门用来评估情商行为的潜力（或能力）。它采用的方法与本书中许多其他心理测试工具非常不同。

测试作者声明，他们的模型将情商定义为运用推理能力和与情绪有关的能力，以及为了达到最佳表现，思考和感受协调作用的能力。

MSCEIT 模型由以下**情绪蓝图**组成：
1. **情绪识别**：你和其他人正在体验什么样的情绪？
2. **情绪利用**：这些情绪如何引导注意力、影响思考？
3. **情绪理解**：什么引起了这些情绪，它们可能会怎样变化？
4. **情绪管理**：什么情绪策略能够最好地解决这个问题？

版权归 MHS 多重健康系统有限公司，经允许使用。

TESTING FOR PERSONAL DEVELOPMENT

EI ABILITY TEST

THE MSCEIT EMOTIONAL INTELLIGENCE TEST

How we handle our emotions, whether in one to one situations, in a team, or in the boardroom is very important to an individual's success in the workplace.

David Caruso, one of the authors of the MSCEIT quotes directly:

> *"You can ask a client to provide a self-estimate of their emotional abilities, and they will gladly comply with your request. The problem is that these confident self-assessments are often at times dead wrong. Because the MSCEIT is like an objective test, an IQ test for emotions, many people are surprised and sometimes upset by their results. Some clients have completely dismissed the entire notion of EI, as they struggle with their assessment results. That's when we examine their scores, and note, with a sense of irony, very low scores on their ability to effectively manage emotions."*
>
> **David Caruso (Mayer, Salovey & Caruso Emotional Intelligence Test - 2007)**

Notes

_____

_____

_____

_____

_____

个人发展测试

EI 能力测试

MSCEIT 情绪智力测试

无论是一对一，还是在团队或董事会中，如何处理自己的情绪对于职场上个人的成功都非常重要。

MSCEIT 的编写者之一大卫·克鲁索直接引述道：

> "你可以让客户提供对自己情绪能力的自我评估，并且他们会欣然照做。问题是这些自信满满的自我评估往往是完全错误的。MSCEIT 就像一个客观的、针对情绪的 IQ 测试，许多人会对自己的结果感到吃惊甚至沮丧。因为抗拒自己的评估结果，一些客户彻底放弃了整个 EI 概念。具有讽刺意味的是，这个时候，看看他们的得分，就会发现他们有效管理情绪的能力得分很低。"
>
> **大卫·克鲁索（梅耶，萨洛维 & 克鲁索 情商测试—2007）**

TESTING FOR PERSONAL DEVELOPMENT

EI ABILITY TEST

EXAMPLE OF THE MSCEIT

Here is an example of the MSCEIT type items in the questionnaire. See what responses you might come up with yourself:

Q1. Perceiving Emotions

What emotions are expressed by this face?

	Low				High
Happiness	1	2	3	4	5
Fear	1	2	3	4	5

Answer: Happiness, surely, but the ratings will vary. Ours was 4!

Notes

个人发展测试

EI 能力测试

MSCEIT 举例

这里有个问卷中 MSCEIT 类型题目的例子。看看自己可能会怎么回答。

问题 1. 情绪感知

这张脸表现的是什么情绪?

	低				高
快乐	1	2	3	4	5
恐惧	1	2	3	4	5

答案：当然是快乐，但是评分可能是不固定的，我们的得分是 4！

版权归 MHS 多重健康系统有限公司，经允许使用。

TESTING FOR PERSONAL DEVELOPMENT

EI ABILITY TEST

EXAMPLE OF THE MSCEIT

Q2. Using emotions

How helpful would each of these feelings be when proofing a budget for the last time before it is submitted in a contract proposal?

	Not helpful				Very helpful
a. Some tension	1	2	3	4	5
b. Joy	1	2	3	4	5
c. Excitement	1	2	3	4	5

Answer: We answered tension 3, joy 1 and excitement 2.

Notes

_____

_____

_____

_____

_____

个人发展测试

EI 能力测试

MSCEIT 举例

问题 2. 情绪利用

> 最后一次核对预算并准备放进合同建议书时，
> 下面这些感受分别有多大帮助？
>
> | | 没有帮助 | | | 非常有帮助 | |
> |---|---|---|---|---|---|
> | a. 有些紧张 | 1 | 2 | 3 | 4 | 5 |
> | b. 高兴 | 1 | 2 | 3 | 4 | 5 |
> | c. 兴奋 | 1 | 2 | 3 | 4 | 5 |

我们的答案是：紧张为 3，快乐为 1，兴奋为 2。

TESTING FOR PERSONAL DEVELOPMENT

EI ABILITY TEST

EXAMPLE OF THE MSCEIT

Q3. Understanding emotions

A feeling of contempt most closely combines the emotions of (select one):

a. Surprise and anger

b. Anger and fear

c. Anxiety and fear

d. Disgust and anger

e. Hatred and guilt

Answer: We answered d. as the closest, because disgust seems to fit but not necessarily anger.

Notes

个人发展测试

EI 能力测试

MSCEIT 举例

问题 3. 情绪理解

鄙视的感觉和下面哪种情绪关系最紧密
（选择一个）：

a. 惊讶和气愤
b. 气愤和恐惧
c. 焦虑和恐惧
d. 厌恶和气愤 ✓
e. 憎恨和内疚

答案：我们选择 d 是最接近的，厌恶很符合，但不一定气愤。

TESTING FOR PERSONAL DEVELOPMENT

EI ABILITY TEST
EXAMPLE OF THE MSCEIT

Q4. Managing emotions

A manager received sad news. He wants to feel happy before attending an important client meeting. How helpful is each of these in getting him to feel happy:

	Not helpful			Very helpful	
Listen to sad music to calm down	1	2	3	4	5
Review his accomplishments	1	2	3	4	5
Sit alone in his office	1	2	3	4	5

Answer: We leave you to make your own mind up for this question!

Notes

_____

_____

_____

_____

_____

个人发展测试

EI 能力测试

MSCEIT 举例

问题 4. 情绪管理

一名经理收到了不好的消息，他想在出席重要的客户会议之前能高兴些，下面这些哪一个有助于让他高兴起来：

	没有帮助			非常有帮助	
听悲伤的音乐，平静下来	1	2	3	4	5
回顾自己的成就	1	2	3	4	5
独自坐在办公室	1	2	3	4	5

答案：我们让您自己决定答案！

版权归 MHS 多重健康系统有限公司，经允许使用。

TESTING FOR PERSONAL DEVELOPMENT

EI ABILITY TEST

CASE STUDY: MSCEIT RESULTS

In Andrew's case the results provided confirmation and clarification of the issues involved in his management skills. The chart shows that he was fairly competent at **perceiving** (Perceiving Emotions) how his staff felt, and was extremely skilled at **understanding** why they felt as they did and how their feelings changed from day to day (Understanding Emotions). However, he was not integrating this emotional information into his decision making. Instead of **engaging** with the emotions (Using & Managing) he blocked them out.

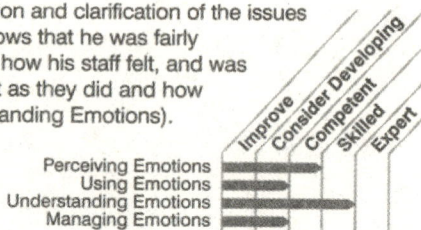

Improve / Consider / Developing / Competent / Skilled / Expert

Perceiving Emotions
Using Emotions
Understanding Emotions
Managing Emotions

The MSCEIT results provided Andrew with both the insight and the process by which he could enhance his management style; helping him use his own emotions more when talking with his people, eg *'Well I don't want to move either, but I'm sure that once I've solved my journey problems, working in the new building will be much more peaceful'.*

Andrew received coaching to develop the way he managed his own emotions when making decisions, eg working with uncertainty in a less predictable environment.

Notes

个人发展测试

EI 能力测试

案例研究：MSCEIT 结果

安德鲁案例的结果肯定并清楚地表明了他在管理技能上的问题，表格显示，他比较能够**感知**（情绪感知）到员工的感受，非常能**理解**为什么他们有那样的感受和这些感受每一天的变化（情绪理解）。但是，他并没有把这些情绪信息融入到决策中，不是**处理**情绪（情绪利用＆管理）而是排除掉情绪。

MSCEIT 结果为安德鲁提供了改善管理风格的分析和过程，帮助他与队员交谈时更多利用自己的情绪，例如：

"好吧，我也不想调过去，但是我相信只要解决了通勤问题，在新的地点工作会安静得多。"

安德鲁接受了教练，培养做决策时管理自己情绪的方法，例如，在不可预测的环境里处理不确定性。

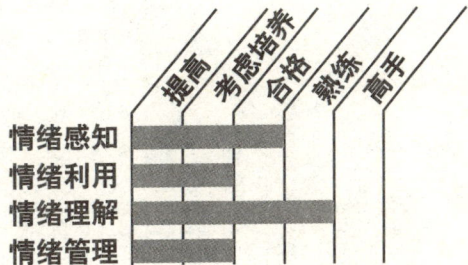

TESTING FOR CAREER COUNSELLING
职业咨询测试

TESTING FOR CAREER COUNSELLING

INTERESTS & VALUES INVENTORIES

So far we have discussed how aptitude, personality and emotional intelligence tests help the individual develop a heightened self-awareness. We will now highlight how using a career interests and values inventory can help an individual focus on areas for career exploration. Psychometric tests can give us an informed perspective on our strengths and weaknesses, allowing us to focus on any new skills needed.

As part of an in-depth careers interview it is beneficial to use a **combination** of different tests, allowing greater self-understanding of the individual, eg:

- **Aptitude tests** which measure your ability for particular types of activity or ways of thinking, and identify any special talent for a certain type of job, eg numerical aptitude for accountancy
- **Personality tests** designed to find out how you might react in certain situations
- **Emotional Intelligence tests** which measure certain behaviours relating to how you manage your own emotions and those of others around you
- **Interests and Values Inventories** which help with an individual's self perceptions and career aspirations. They tend to look at areas such as: preferred working style, career development and career direction

> *'What is necessary to change a person is to change his awareness of himself'*
> **Abraham Maslow**

Notes

_____

_____

_____

_____

_____

職業咨询测试

兴趣 & 价值观量表

　　到这里为止，我们已经讲过能力倾向、人格和情商测试如何帮助个人培养敏锐的自我意识。接下来我们来看如何利用职业兴趣和价值观量表，帮助个人进行职业探索。心理测试能为我们提供有用的角度来观察优势和弱势，从而让我们关注需要的新技能。

　　作为深入的职业面谈的一部分，使用不同测试的**组合**，有助于个人更多地了解自我，例如：

　　·**能力倾向测试，**测试的是你在某种具体活动类型或思考方式方面的能力，并且能识别出某个工作类型需要的特殊才能，如会计师的数理能力。

　　·**性格测试，**用来发现你在某种情境中可能产生的反应。

　　·**情商测试，**测试的是关于如何管理自己和周围人情绪的某些行为。

　　·**兴趣和价值观量表，**有助于自我认知和了解职业理想，它们倾向于观察以下这些领域，如：工作方式偏好，职业发展和职业方向。

> "改变一个人需要
> 改变他的自我意识"
> ——亚伯拉罕·马斯洛

TESTING FOR CAREER COUNSELLING

INTERESTS & VALUES INVENTORIES
CASE STUDY: STRONG INTEREST INVENTORY® (SII) TOOL

Samantha, who was 24, had worked in various casual jobs in pubs and restaurants since leaving school. She was unhappy and very confused about what type of job she would be most suited to. She made an appointment to see a qualified career consultant who was licensed to administer a range of psychometric tests and would be able to aid her in exploring different career options.

As part of Samantha's career exploration she was asked to complete the **Strong Interest Inventory® (SII) tool**. The inventory, originally developed in the 1920s and subsequently revised, is used worldwide. It is backed up by decades of research with people who are satisfied in their careers. The current version is based on the ideas of John Holland.

The best way to use Interest Inventories is as a guide to possibilities only. We cannot emphasise enough how important it is to research any career interests, speak to someone already doing that job to see if it is really what you want to do, and where possible undertake work experience or work shadowing. Research shows that people are most productive in work that they enjoy doing.

Strong Interest Inventory is a registered trademark of CPP, Inc. Used with permission

Notes

职业咨询测试

兴趣 & 价值观量表

案例研究：斯特朗兴趣量表（SII）工具

自从毕业后，24 岁的萨曼莎在酒吧、饭店做过各种各样的临时工。她很不快乐，不知道自己最适合的工作类型是什么。她预约了一名专业的、有认证资格进行心理测试的职业咨询师，来帮助自己探索不同的职业选择。

作为职业探索的一部分，她被要求完成**斯特朗兴趣量表（SII）工具**。这个量表最初创立于 20 世纪 20 年代，经过不断修改，现在已在全球广泛使用。这份量表得到了数十年来对满意自己职业的人的调查研究的证实。目前的版本基于约翰·霍兰德的研究。

利用兴趣量表的最佳方式是仅仅把它作为一种可能性的引导。研究你的任何职业兴趣，与已经做那份工作的人交谈，看看你是否真正想做，可能的话，着手体验下那份工作，这些非常重要，再怎么强调也不为过。研究表明，人们在从事自己喜欢的工作时工作效率最高。

斯特朗兴趣量表是 CPP 有限公司注册商标。经允许使用。

TESTING FOR CAREER COUNSELLING

INTERESTS & VALUES INVENTORIES

CAREER INTEREST INVENTORIES

Most of us have limited knowledge of the range of jobs that exist even within our own occupational arena. This is why using an Interest Inventory is of value to those who already have some idea of where they want to work as well as to individuals who do not know where to start.

Career Interest Inventories encourage people to think about the world of work and the areas that interest them the most. For instance they:

- Identify career options consistent with interests
- Highlight career options that haven't been considered
- Choose appropriate education and training routes relevant to interests
- Help maintain a balance between work and leisure activities
- Understand a preferred learning environment
- Learn about preferences for leadership, risk taking, and teamwork
- Use interests in shaping career directions
- Decide on a work oriented focus for the future
- Provide an insight into aspects of the world of work

Notes

职业咨询测试

兴趣 & 价值观量表

职业兴趣量表

大多数人对于现存的工作类型，甚至自己的职业领域中存在的工作类型，只有有限的了解。因此，对于那些不知道从哪里起步和已经有些想法的人来说，使用兴趣量表很有帮助。

职业兴趣量表鼓励人们思考工作领域和最吸引他们的领域。例如，它们能：

- 识别出符合你兴趣的职业选择
- 显示出你没有考虑到的职业选择
- 选择与兴趣有关的合适的教育和培训路径
- 帮助你保持工作和业余活动的平衡
- 弄清楚你偏好的学习环境
- 使你了解自己关于领导力、承担风险和团队合作的偏好
- 利用兴趣塑造职业方向
- 决定未来的工作重点
- 提供对工作领域方方面面的深刻分析

TESTING FOR CAREER COUNSELLING.

INTERESTS & VALUES INVENTORIES
STRONG INTEREST INVENTORY® (SII) TOOL

John Holland's (1959) model of fit between work environments and the individual provides a unifying framework or model of six occupational themes into which most jobs fit. The newly revised Strong Interest Inventory® tool puts focus on business and technology careers.

Holland's six occupational themes

Theme	Interests	Work activities
Realistic	Mechanical, tools, outdoors	Operating equipment, using tools, building, repairing
Investigative	Science, theories, ideas, data	Lab work, problem solving, researching, analysing
Artistic	Self-expression, art appreciation	Composing music, drama, writing, creating visual art, cooking

Continued →

Notes

_____

_____

_____

_____

_____

職業咨询测试

兴趣 & 价值观量表

斯特朗兴趣量表® (SII) 工具

约翰·霍兰德的工作环境和个人的匹配模型（1959）提供了一个统一的框架，或者说适合大部分工作的六种职业主题模型。最新修订的斯特朗兴趣量表®关注的是商业和科技职业。

霍兰德的六种职业主题

主题	兴趣	工作活动
现实型	机械，工具，户外	操作设备，使用工具，建筑，修理
研究型	科学，理论，想法，数据	实验室工作，解决问题，研究，分析
艺术型	自我表达，艺术欣赏	作曲，戏剧，写作，视觉艺术创作，烹饪

续表 →

斯特朗兴趣量表是 CPP 有限公司注册商标。经允许使用。

TESTING FOR CAREER COUNSELLING.

INTERESTS & VALUES INVENTORIES
STRONG INTEREST INVENTORY® (SII) TOOL

Holland's six occupational themes (continued)

Theme	Interests	Work activities
Social	People, teamwork, helping others, community service	Teaching, explaining, instructing, care giving
Enterprising	Business, politics, leadership, influence	Selling, persuading, managing
Conventional	Organisation, data, finance	Setting up procedures, organising, processing data

Notes

_____

_____

_____

_____

_____

职业咨询测试

兴趣 & 价值观量表

斯特朗兴趣量表® (SII) 工具

霍兰德的六种职业主题（续）

主题	兴趣	工作活动
社会型	人，团队合作，帮助他人，社区服务	教授，解释，指导，给予关爱
企业型	商业，政治，领导力，影响	销售，说服，管理
常规型	组织，数据，金融	设置程序，组织，处理数据

斯特朗兴趣量表是 CPP 有限公司注册商标。经允许使用。

TESTING FOR CAREER COUNSELLING

INTERESTS & VALUES INVENTORIES

CASE STUDY: STRONG INTEREST INVENTORY® (SII) TOOL RESULTS

Having completed the inventory, Samantha's Strong Interest Career themes came out (in order of strength) as:

1. **Social** – people oriented, teamworker, helping, teaching, caring for others.
2. **Conventional** – organisation, data management, setting up procedures, keeping records.

Her top occupational preferences, as indicated by the SII, were nursing and social care.

It became clear during the feedback session, and from her work history, that Samantha was very sociable and outgoing. Meeting and helping others was something she really enjoyed. However, the social side was no longer enough for her: she had begun to realise that a career was important. The next issue to explore was her values.

The values that we each hold influence how we deal with everyday tasks both inside and outside the workplace. Exploring an individual's values in a development, teambuilding or career counselling situation can lead to an understanding and resolution of problem areas, the development of stronger teams and the clarification of career goals. The SPV questionnaire (see next page) was used to explore Samantha's values, both personally and interpersonally.

Strong Interest Inventory is a registered trademark of CPP, Inc. Used with permission

Notes

_____

_____

_____

_____

_____

職业咨询测试

兴趣 & 价值观量表

案例研究：斯特朗兴趣量表® (SII) 工具结果

完成量表后，萨曼莎的斯特朗兴趣职业主题结果（按照由强到弱的程度）如下：

1. **社会型**——以人为导向，团队协作者，帮助，教导，关怀他人
2. **常规型**——组织，数据管理，设置程序，记录

如同 SII 所示，她最偏向的职业是护理和社会关怀工作。

在反馈环节，这一点变得更加清晰。从她的工作经历来看，萨曼莎很善于交际，性格外向，接触和帮助他人让她乐在其中。但是，她已经不能满足于社会型那一面：她开始意识到职业的重要性。下一个要探索的问题就是她的价值观。

价值观会影响到我们如何处理职场内外的日常事务。在发展、团队建设或职业咨询的情境下，探索一个人的价值观有助于了解并找出问题的解决方案，培养更强大的团队和厘清职业目标。我们使用 SPV 量表(见下一页)从个人和人际两方面来探索萨曼莎的价值观。

斯特朗兴趣量表是 CPP 有限公司注册商标。经允许使用。

TESTING FOR CAREER COUNSELLING

INTERESTS & VALUES INVENTORIES

GORDON'S SURVEYS OF PERSONAL & INTERPERSONAL VALUES (SPV & SIV)

Survey of Personal Values (SPV)

Leonard V Gordon started research into personality in 1953, before moving on to look at the values we hold that influence how we deal with everyday tasks and people both inside and outside the workplace. Exploring an individual's values in a counselling situation can lead to an understanding and resolution of problem areas like the clarification of life or career goals.

The SPV is designed to measure certain critical values that help determine the manner in which individuals cope with the problems of everyday living:

1. **Practical mindedness** – likes practical things, material – and economically – minded.
2. **Achievement** – values growth, accomplishment, enjoys challenge and effort.
3. **Variety** – prefers a range of activity, dislikes routine, prefers new experiences.
4. **Decisiveness** – values and sticks to own opinions, likes thinking through decisions.
5. **Orderliness** – prefers organisation, routine and schedules.
6. **Goal orientation** – prefers clear objectives and seeing tasks to completion.

Used with the kind permission of ASE.

Notes

職業咨询测试

兴趣 & 价值观量表

戈登的个人 & 人际价值观调查 (SPV&SIV)

个人价值观调查 (SPV)

莱昂纳德·戈登于 1953 年开始研究性格，后来研究价值观对人们处理职场内外日常事务的影响。在咨询情境下，探索个人的价值观能帮助我们了解问题所在，找到解决方案，如明确生活目标或职业目标。

SPV 是为了测试某些重大的价值观，这些价值观决定个人在处理日常生活中的问题时所采取的方式：

1. **实际意识**——喜欢实际的事物，关注物质和经济
2. **成就**——注重成长，成就，享受挑战和奋斗
3. **多样化**——偏爱多种活动，不喜欢常规工作，喜欢新的体验
4. **决断**——重视并坚持己见，喜欢决策思考
5. **条理**——偏好组织，常规工作和行程安排
6. **目标导向**——偏好清晰的目标和看到任务完成

经 ASE 允许使用。

TESTING FOR CAREER COUNSELLING

INTERESTS & VALUES INVENTORIES

GORDON'S SURVEYS OF PERSONAL & INTERPERSONAL VALUES (SPV & SIV)

Survey of Interpersonal Values (SIV)

The SIV is designed to measure certain values involving the individual's personal, social, marital and occupational adjustment:

1. **Support** – values kindness, encouragement and consideration from others.
2. **Conformity** – doing the correct thing, following regulation.
3. **Recognition** – being looked up to, considered important, admired.
4. **Independence** – doing what one wants, making own decisions.
5. **Benevolence** – doing things for others, sharing, helping those in need.
6. **Leadership** – being in charge, having authority, power.

Used with the kind permission of ASE.

Notes

_____

_____

_____

_____

_____

职业咨询测试

兴趣 & 价值观量表

戈登的个人 & 人际价值观调查（SPV&SIV）

人际价值观调查（SIV）

SIV 是为了测试涉及个体的个人、社会、婚姻和职业调整的价值观。

1. **支持**——重视来自他人的友善、鼓励和体贴
2. **顺从**——做正确的事，循规蹈矩
3. **认可**——被尊敬，被重视，受人钦佩
4. **独立**——做想做的事，自己做决定
5. **仁爱**——为他人做事，分享，帮助需要帮助的人
6. **领导**——掌管，有权威，权力

经 ASE 允许使用。

TESTING FOR CAREER COUNSELLING

INTERESTS & VALUES INVENTORIES
GORDON'S SURVEYS OF PERSONAL
& INTERPERSONAL VALUES (SPV & SIV)

By using the Gordon Survey of Personal and Interpersonal Values questionnaire Samantha was helped to delve deeper into her individual value system. She found that she:

- Valued growth and challenge and an occupation that involved variety
- Valued recognition and the need to feel in charge

This extra self-understanding was discussed with her career counsellor. The job areas of nursing and social work were highlighted as areas for further investigation and research. Training would be required in both these roles.

Following career counselling it was strongly recommended that she also spoke to people already working in those jobs and to tutors about the course content and whether she had the correct qualifications. The outcome was that Samantha decided to explore nursing as a career.

Used with the kind permission of ASE.

Notes

职业咨询测试

兴趣 & 价值观量表

戈登的个人 & 人际价值观调查（SPV&SIV）

　　使用戈登的个人和人际价值观调查量表帮助萨曼莎深入剖析了她的个人价值观体系，她发现自己：

- 重视成长、挑战以及有变化的职业
- 重视认可和对掌控感的需求

　　同职业咨询师谈论了以上增加的自我了解后，护理和社会工作被列为需要进一步调查和研究的领域，她需要接受这两个职业角色的培训。

　　后续的职业咨询中，强烈建议和已经在这些领域工作的人们交谈，和导师谈谈课程内容以及她是否具备合适的资格。结果是萨曼莎决定选择护理作为职业。

　　经 ASE 允许使用。

USEFUL INFORMATION

实用信息

TESTING ONLINE

Online psychometric test administration is proving to be a very popular choice for assessing individuals and nowadays tends to be preferred to paper and pencil based test administration.

For multinational organisations that may wish to test individuals in different countries in, say, the space of an afternoon, the fact that tests can be completed over the internet makes online testing of enormous practical benefit. In addition, many tests are now available in multiple languages (eg the Expert Testing System used by Thomas International (DISC) is available in over 50 languages), making testing online very accessible to different cultures across different continents.

However, there are advantages and disadvantages to testing online which the test user needs to be made aware of.

Notes

实用信息

在线测试

在线心理测试已被证明是深受欢迎的评估个人的方式，目前比纸笔测试更受欢迎。

对于希望在某个下午测试在不同国家的不同个人的跨国公司来说，可以通过因特网完成测试具有很大的实用价值。此外，现在许多测试有多种语言（例如，托马斯国际（DISC）使用的专家测试系统有50多种语言），不同大陆不同文化的人都能进行在线测试。

但是，在线测试既有优点也有缺点，受测试者需要意识到这一点。

TESTING ONLINE
ADVANTAGES

The advantages of online testing for both test takers and test users are:

- **Cost effective** – cuts out the assessment centre where test takers would normally be called to sit a paper and pencil test. Instead the individual can complete the test from their own laptop or computer
- **Secure** – the test taker is provided, by the test administrator, with a confidential login and password. This directs the test taker to a secure, online assessment site, owned by the test distributor
- **More flexible** – test takers can complete an array of tests around the globe. Online assessment site test access is normally available 7 days a week, 24 hours a day
- **No paper** – there is no need to carry large amounts of paperwork with you
- **Quick turnaround** – when the test taker has completed an online test the administrator will be notified, normally via email. The test administrator then accesses the online assessment site, locates the test taker's report and scores it electronically. The report is produced in a PDF format in a matter of seconds. Alternatively, scoring can be done by a scoring bureau which then forwards the scored report to the test administrator

Notes

实用信息

在线测试

优势

对于测试使用者和测试对象，在线测试的优势是：

• **节约成本**——省去了测试对象进行纸笔测试的评估中心，相反，个人可以在自己的笔记本或计算机上完成测试。

• **安全**——测试管理员给测试对象提供保密的用户名和密码，测试对象凭此进入安全的、属于测试经销商的在线评估站点。

• **更灵活**——测试对象能够在全球各地完成一系列测试。在线评估站点的测试通常一周 7 天、一天 24 小时都能访问。

• **无纸化**——不需要携带大量的纸质文件。

• **周转迅速**——测试对象完成在线测试后，通常测试管理员会收到邮件通知，然后管理员进入在线测试站点，找到测试对象的报告，进行电子打分。几秒之内，就能生成 PDF 格式的报告。或者，通过评分机构进行计分，再把打过分的报告转发给测试管理员。

TESTING ONLINE

DISADVANTAGES

- **Verification** of test taker – are they who they say they are?
- **Distractions** – when the test administrator sends instructions, it is beneficial to provide the test taker with some guidelines on appropriate times to complete the test, ie free from other distractions and with sufficient time available to answer as accurately as possible. They should choose a time when they are not too stressed or tired, not influenced by alcohol, and definitely not asking friends for help: 'Er Geoff ...do you think this is me?'
- **Ability tests** – the test taker may cheat, using the internet for help in formulating answers
- **Feedback** – It is always good practice to provide feedback. There is nothing worse than for the test taker to complete an assessment and then just receive, by email, a PDF electronically scored report, produced by an Expert System with no other feedback, particularly when the results are not that flattering, or the test taker is thinking: 'this isn't me!' Face to face feedback is best but if this is not possible, telephone or video conferencing are acceptable alternatives
- **Language interpretation** – misunderstandings of translation can occur because there is nobody to verify translation
- **First language** – tests should be in the test taker's native language to avoid language misinterpretation

Notes

_____

_____

_____

_____

_____

実用信息

在线测试

劣势

· **核实**测试对象——他们是自己所声称的那个人吗？

· **分散注意力**——测试管理员发送指令时，给测试对象提供一些关于如何在恰当的时间来完成测试的指导原则是很有帮助的，即不要受到其他事务干扰，尽量在时间充分的情况下尽可能准确地回答问题。要选择不太紧张或疲惫、不受到酒精影响的状态，绝对不要请朋友帮忙："呃，杰夫，你觉得我是这样吗？"

· **能力测试**——测试对象回答问题时可能会作弊，通过互联网寻求帮助。

· **反馈**——提供反馈常常是好的做法。对于测试对象来说，最糟糕的莫过于完成评估后，只收到一封邮件，里面除了专家系统生成的 PDF 版的电子计分报告外，没有其他反馈，尤其是结果不那么理想时，或者测试对象认为："这不是我！"时。面对面反馈是最好的，如果不行，电话或视频会议也是可接受的选择方式。

· **语言翻译**——因为没有人校验翻译，可能会因翻译引起误解。

· **第一语言**——为了避免语言上的误解，测试语言应当为被测试对象的母语。

GOOD PRACTICE

It is important that the test administration should follow a standardised procedure whether we are measuring personality, ability, aptitudes, motivation or vocational interests. Then we can assume that if all the test takers have been treated similarly, any variation in scores will be within the people and not in the test conditions.

Short-term environmental factors that can affect and possibly reduce test performance are:

- Room lighting
- Room temperature
- Noise
- Distractions
- Time of day
- Attitude of test administrator
- Illness on the day

Test users **can** control the above.

Notes

_____

_____

_____

_____

_____

实用信息

良好的做法

　　无论测试的是性格、能力、能力倾向、动机还是职业兴趣，都应该遵循标准化的步骤实施测试，这一点很重要。然后我们可以认为，如果所有的测试对象都受到相同的对待，那么任何分数的变化都是由于人的不同而不是测试环境引起的。

　　能够影响或可能降低测试表现的短期环境因素有：

- 房间的光线
- 房间的温度
- 噪音
- 干扰
- 一天中的不同时间段
- 测试管理员的态度
- 当天是否生病

测试使用者**能够**控制以上因素。

GOOD PRACTICE

Long-term environmental factors that can affect and possibly reduce test performance are:

- Parental influence, upbringing
- Quality of education
- Cultural background
- Illness or disability

Test users **cannot** control the above but may be aware of how they may affect test results.

Notes

_____

_____

_____

_____

_____

实用信息

良好的做法

能够影响或可能降低测试表现的长期环境因素有：

- 父母的影响，家教
- 教育质量
- 文化背景
- 疾病或残疾

测试使用者**不能**控制以上因素，但是能意识到它们对测试结果会产生什么影响。

STANDARDS IN TESTING, TRAINING & CERTIFICATION

The British Psychological Society has devised a certification scheme to train people in the proper use of occupational tests. The Certificates of Competence in Occupational Testing (Levels A/B/B+/Full) are delivered by assessors who must be chartered psychologists. The main benefits of the scheme are that it provides:

- A clear specification of what the potential test user needs to know and be able to do, to use tests properly
- Access to most ability and aptitude tests, interest inventories and career guidance materials
- Evidence of qualifications which should be 'transferable' between various providers of training in testing and between various publishers and other suppliers of test materials
- A form of national certification of competence in occupational testing which employers will be encouraged to recognise for the proper use of psychological testing within their organisations. If employers stipulate that testing may only be carried out by or under the direction of suitably qualified people, professional standards in testing should improve

A code of good practice is available from the Psychological Testing Centre www.psychtesting.org.uk

Notes

_____

_____

_____

_____

_____

实用信息

测试、培训 & 证明的标准

　　英国心理学会制定了一个认证计划，用来培训人们正确使用职业测试。职业能力测试证书(A/B/B 级 +/ 完全等级)由评审员发放，评审员必须是特许心理学家。 这个认证计划的主要好处是：

• 提供潜在测试用户需要了解和能做的、及正确使用测试的明确说明。

• 提供大部分能力和能力倾向测试、兴趣量表和职业指导材料

• 提供不同测试培训提供者、测试出版商和其他测试材料供应者之间"通用"的资格证明

• 提供全国职业测试能力证明，鼓励老板认可组织内部正确使用心理测试。如果雇主规定必须由专业人员实施或指导实施测试，就能提高测试的专业标准。

　　通过心理测试中心可获取良好做法准则　www.psychtesting.org.uk。

USEFUL INFORMATION

CONCLUSION

We have introduced the reader to psychometric testing as generally applied in the workplace. Starting with selection testing, we have then moved on to show how testing can also be useful in developing organisations, teams and individuals. Testing has been shown to be of prime importance in career counselling, mainly to direct personality and ability strengths towards choosing a career compatible with personality traits, values and aspirations. Job satisfaction is a powerful ingredient in successful performance and well-being in the workplace.

We recommend that organisations write a policy for good practice in occupational testing and follow guidelines recommended by the British Psychological Society Psychological Test Centre.

The authors would like to stress that the choice of tests and the opinions in this book are their own. We recommend that training in test use is undertaken as a first step, after advice about testing has been sought from experienced psychologists or trained test users.

Notes

_____

_____

_____

_____

_____

实用信息

结束语

　　我们向读者介绍了职场上通常会用到的心理测试，从遴选测试到证明测试如何帮助组织、团队和个人发展。测试在职业咨询时至关重要，能帮助人们根据人格和能力优势做出与人格特征、价值观和愿望相一致的职业选择。工作满意感是职场中取得卓越表现和获得幸福感的重要组成部分。

　　我们建议企业制定关于职业测试的良好操作政策，遵照英国心理学会测试中心所提供的准则。

　　作者要强调的是，本书所选择的测试及观点均来自本人。我们建议您在咨询过经验丰富的心理学家和受过训练的测试使用者后，把接受如何使用测试的培训作为第一步。

实用信息

延伸阅读 & 参考书目

Bar-On EQ-i
Multi-Health Systems Inc, Toronto, Canada and the United Kingdom www.mhs.com
Dr Reuven Bar-On www.reuvenbaron.org

Belbin Team Roles,
Belbin Associates, Cambridge, United Kingdom www.belbin.com

Certificates of Competence (Level A & B) in
Occupational Testing www.psychtesting.org.uk

ECCOS
(Eysenck, Cripps, Cook Occupational Scales): A User's Guide, Cook M. and Cripps B.D. 2007
www.eccos.co.uk

EQ 360 Multi-Rater Feedback
Multi-Health Systems Inc, Toronto, Canada and the United Kingdom www.mhs.com

General Ability Tests (GAT2)
ASE Human Capital Consulting, London www.ase-solutions.co.uk

Gordon's SPV & SIV
ASE Human Capital Consulting, London www.ase-solutions.co.uk

Mayer, Salovey, Caruso Emotional Intelligence Tool
Multi-Health Systems Inc, Toronto, Canada and the United Kingdom www.mhs.com

Myers-Briggs Type Indicator®
Oxford Psychologists Press (OPP) Oxford, United Kingdom www.opp.eu.com and Consulting
Psychologists Press (CPP) Palo Alto, California www.cpp.com

Personal Profile Analysis (PPA)
Thomas International of Marlow, UK. www.thomasinternational.net

SHL Motivational Questionnaire
SHL Group Ltd. SHL is a registered trade mark of SHL Group Ltd www.shl.com

实用信息

延伸阅读 & 参考书目

Strong Interest Inventory® (SII) (newly revised) Consulting Psychologists Press (CPP) Palo Alto, California www.cpp.com

Saville Consulting Wave®
www.savilleconsulting.com MacIver R, Saville P, Kurz R, Mitchener A, Mariscal K, Parry G, Becker S, Saville W, O'Connor K, Patterson R & Oxley H (2006). *Making Waves – Saville Consulting Wave Styles questionnaires. Selection & Development Review*, 22 (2), pp 17-23.

W-GCTA
Watson G. and Glaser M. (2002) Watson-Glaser Critical Thinking Appraisal UK Edition. The Psychological Corporation, London. www.harcourt-uk.com

Quality of Working Life Questionnaire
ASE Human Capital Consulting, London www.ase-solutions.co.uk

16PF Oxford Psychologists Press (OPP) Oxford, United Kingdom www.opp.eu.com

BOOKS AND JOURNALS

Emotional Intelligence, Goleman D, Bantam Books, 1995

The EQ Edge, Emotional Intelligence and Your Success, Stein S.J (Ph.D) and Howard E.B (M.D),

Jossey-Bass 2000 and 2006 revised, www.mhs.com

Working with Emotional Intelligence, Goleman D, Bloomsbury Publishing, 1998

Psychological Assessment in the Workplace – A Manager's Guide, Cook M. and Cripps B.D, John Wiley & Sons, 2005

A Theory of Vocational Choice, Holland J.L, Journal of Counselling Psychology,1959, spr, vol 6 (1) 35-45

Emotions of Normal People, Marston W.M, Routledge, 2002

作者简介

巴里·克里普斯博士

巴里·克里普斯博士是一名注册职业心理学家，是工业、商业、高等教育和体育行业的独立咨询师。他的研究领域是高管培训及组织的学习、发展和评估。曾担任过培训董事会主要成员，顶级商学院校外人力资源主考人，英国特许人事和发展协会 (CIPD) 顾问及英国皇家心理学会能力测试审核官。

联系方式　网址：www.performance-psychology.com
　　　　　　　邮箱：drbarrycripps@btinternet.com

多萝西·斯普赖

多萝西·斯普赖是一名商业心理学家，为来自公共和私营机构的广大客户提供服务。她的研究领域是培养员工和客户忠诚度，国际在线心理测试计分和阐释，职业咨询和情绪智力 EQ-I & EQ 360 认证培训和授权。多萝西是 ECCOS 的奠基人之一，也是就业技能指导评估员。在英国和全世界均有她的自我意识提升工作坊，也曾在罗马尼亚、迪拜、荷兰和纽约多次讲学。曾获得英国总理培训发展国家培训奖 (2007 年)。

联系方式　网址：www.careerperformance.co.uk
　　　　　　　邮箱：dorothy@careerperformance.co.uk

英汉对照管理丛书

英汉对照管理袖珍手册